HEALING THE
WOUNDED HEART

AND

PERSONAL
MINISTRY GUIDE

Removing Obstacles to Intimacy With God

THOM GARDNER

HEALING THE WOUNDED HEART

Removing Obstacles to Intimacy With God

Please note that all the names of people who were ministered to and who are mentioned in this book have been altered, along with key locations and some details. This is for the protection of their privacy and confidentiality, without which healing cannot take place.

Destiny Image® Publishers, Inc.
P.O. Box 310
Shippensburg, PA 17257-0310

"Speaking to the Purposes of God for this Generation
and for the Generations to Come"

ISBN 0-7684-2326-0

For Worldwide Distribution
Printed in the U.S.A.

This book and all other Destiny Image, Revival Press, MercyPlace, Fresh Bread, Destiny Image Fiction, and Treasure House books are available at Christian bookstores and distributors worldwide.

For a U.S. bookstore nearest you, call **1-800-722-6774**.
For more information on foreign distributors, call **717-532-3040**.
Or reach us on the Internet:
www.destinyimage.com

CONTENTS

AUTHOR'S PREFACE

This book is intended to be used as a personal study that leads to the healing of wounded emotions and brings the reader into a greater intimacy with God. It is not an all inclusive "training manual" for facilitation of total inner healing. Readers with serious life-controlling emotional issues should not rely on this book alone for healing, but should seek out additional competent help from others who have been trained in the ministry of inner healing.

This book includes a reference list for further study. I encourage those who want to administer inner healing to seek thorough training through Grace and Truth Fellowship, Inc., which provides local churches with basic training in the ministry of inner healing (www.Graceandtruthfellowship.com/717-263-6869), or Cornerstone Bible Institute and Seminary (www.Corner stonenet.org / 540-432-2355), or some other recognized source of equipping in the ministry of inner healing.

There are many different approaches to inner healing available throughout the Body of Christ. In writing this book, it is my desire to see you healed and whole, living in the abundant life to which you have been called through Jesus Christ.

FOREWORD

Most of us spend a considerable portion of our adult lives trying to come to terms with what has happened to us in the past. Our prayers, our repentance, and our desires all seem to focus on what life would be like if only "that incident" would not have happened, or if only that gaping emotional wound in our heart could be healed once and for all. But this kind of living must come to an end. If we truly desire a serious and continuous growth in our walk with the Lord, we must realize that dragging around all that stuff from our past eventually becomes too much to bear, too much to keep track of, and definitely too much to fit into God's plan for our lives.

Trying to survive, we have discovered a hundred ways to cover the pain and ignore the haunting images and feelings that follow us everywhere we try to live. We've tried painting them over with religious activity. We've tried to deny them by anesthetizing ourselves with new highs of emotion. We've tried to rebuke them, cast them out, pray them away, sing and dance them away. But when the music is over, when the lights are turned off, we find ourselves hurting with the same intensity as before, wondering if there really will be healing for the things that happened so long ago.

I understand. It is not that we try to ignore the pain. Certainly it is often so intense that it consumes us as though it happened just today. It is not as though we try to cover it. The pain has been too hard for too long. We know better. The pain is there even with a cover over it. We have tried that way out. It is not that we try to deny that it exists or deny that the event ever happened. Repentance seems to be a minute-by-minute experience. We are totally aware of what we suffer.

But when the sense of His calling to us is greater than the pain, when the hope of His presence draws us forward stronger than our pain draws us backward, we make the decision that somehow, somewhere, this has got to end.

And so it can.

There is a place of healing in the Spirit of God, in the personal reality of His presence that the Lord yearns for us to experience. He sees our pain, understands our struggle, and wants nothing more than to bring inner wholeness to His people, to you. This is the genuine place of healing.

Healing the Wounded Heart gives us a biblical and simple approach to use in finding healing for those past hurts. Born out of the author's experience of ministering to thousands around the world, this book has answers, real answers, because it offers healing to the hurting believer.

There is a place of quietness in the heart of God where oil and wine are applied to our hurts.

There is healing in the presence of God.

Don Nori, Publisher
Author, *Secrets of the Most Holy Place*
and *Romancing the Divine*

INTRODUCTION

If you've picked up this book, there is a good chance you have some kind of emotional pain in your life. You may be a housewife who lives in secret dissatisfaction, wondering who you are now that the kids have grown up. Maybe you're the preacher who struggles to feel something, who keeps trudging along simply because you have to—it *is* expected, after all. You could be the homecoming queen who seems to have everything, yet is locked in a battle for approval.

Each of us has some kind of limp in our step as we walk through daily life. We get up in the morning and the limp is not too noticeable—kind of like the limp we might have with a small pebble in our shoe that we don't take the time or effort to figure out how to remove. Then we go to the office and our gait becomes a little stiffer—somehow the pebble seems a little bigger and becomes more irritating; hence, our limp becomes a little more pronounced as we continue to encounter various issues and conflicts. Maybe we go to our Bible study in the evening and leave feeling more guilty and depressed than when we arrived. By the time we get home and throw ourselves into bed, we can hardly walk. That same small pebble in our shoe has seemingly become a boulder. Something has a hold on us—something has compromised our walk.

What are these things that make us limp? They are false beliefs that come up time and time again, like that pebble stuck in our shoe. They determine how we live, where we go, and how we interpret the world around us. They are so much a part of us that we can't remember a time when we didn't limp. Soon we limp without knowing why—it has become automatic.

I remember a story my wife told me about a dog she had when she was younger. Her father once stepped on the dog's paw by accident, and although the dog was not seriously hurt, it occasionally limped as if to elicit sympathy from people by reminding them of what had been done to it in the past. In fact, it would sometimes favor the wrong paw. That dog limped when there seemed to be no real reason, just because of something that had happened long before—which is often exactly what we do.

I've written this book to address the limps in our lives. I have included several instances and illustrations from the lives of the wonderful folks I have ministered to and with—changing the names and specific details, of course, to maintain anonymity. Nevertheless, they are *real* people with *real* problems who have since experienced *real* healing and freedom in Christ.

Several books have been written on the healing of wounded emotions, and I have read and profited from many of them through the years. I have also been the beneficiary of some great teaching by a mentor of mine Pastor Roy Kreider, who spoke the words of life to me that launched my full-time ministry in healing wounded emotions.

So why write another book on inner healing? *Healing the Wounded Heart* does not just present another method for healing; it is based primarily on the exposition of Deuteronomy 7:1-7, which I preached about several years ago, and to which the Lord has added much. The ideas presented are similar to those in other approaches to healing. However, my primary motive for writing this book is to provide a biblical format through which the wounded are brought into an awareness of the presence of God, which enables them to destroy lies and false images by following a simple biblical process.

This is not a psychology book, nor is it a science or a new form of Christian counseling. In fact, it is not a counseling book at all. It is based upon biblical exposition and practical experience gained while ministering healing in a way that focuses on the presence of God, who is the source of all healing. This book exists to provide an opportunity for people to find healing for wounds and limping limitations through a personal encounter with the exalted Christ.

The Bible identifies seven basic influences in Deuteronomy chapter 7, as well as a host of negative emotions that flow from the lies, all of which compromise our inner peace. You will see these basic lies and emotional sets as they affected the lives of regular people in the Bible. Then you will have the opportunity to compare your life to theirs and find the source of the hurt that causes your limping today.

I ask you to read this book in the gentle tone in which it has been written. This is not a book of shouting, but one of whispering in the presence of God—the Lord Himself who is our Healer (see Ex. 15:26).

Behold, I will bring to it health and healing, and I will heal them; and I will reveal to them an abundance of peace and truth (Jeremiah 33:6).

PART ONE

THE NEED FOR
HEALING WOUNDED HEARTS

CHAPTER ONE

"SUFFER THE LITTLE CHILDREN..."

...Jesus...said unto them, Suffer the little children to come unto Me... (Mark 10:14 KJV).

A little boy, perhaps in second or third grade, stands in the middle of his class getting ready to practice for an upcoming Christmas program. The students are full of energy having just come from the playground and are excited thinking about the special occasion when their parents and families will come to hear them sing. With everyone gathered and giggling on the choral risers, the music teacher calls them to attention and the rehearsal begins. The piano sounds the introduction to the first song, and the little boy opens his mouth to sing along with his classmates. He doesn't have much of a voice, but he belts out his monotone offering with the same vigor that he used on the playground a short time earlier. As he attempts to sing the first selection, the look on his teacher's face turns from a pleasing smile to a grimace of disgust. Looking embarrassed, she stops the rehearsal, fixes her gaze on the little boy, and pleads with him in front of the entire class to stop singing. He is the only child who she addresses.

Take a moment and see this picture with the eyes of your heart. Imagine what this boy feels as his teacher throws a wet blanket over him muffling his song. Can you see the little boy who opens his mouth and his heart only to have them closed by one cutting and insensitive remark from a careless teacher? You can almost see his head falling into his chest. This exuberant cherub who only moments earlier was filled with joy now has eyes filling with tears while all other eyes are fixed uncomfortably on him. He is shamed and embarrassed in front of his peers and will be reluctant to open his mouth for the rest of his life to sing a song or offer an opinion for fear of being quenched once again. I wonder what kind of jobs he will consider when he grows up or what kind of children he will raise in his house.

This story is based on an actual event detailed in a healing session at our ministry center. This single "seed event" had great impact for this little boy as he grew into a man who as an adult suffered from panic attacks terrified of any change in his life.

Seeds Are Always Being Sown

This kind of scene is played out in the everyday lives of most folks. Thousands of little, seemingly innocuous events roll past our hearts planting seeds that affect the rest of our days. As a dad, I get a little paranoid about what kinds of seeds I must have planted in my own children. Our words and actions to our children are seeds, and all of us have experienced and sown both good and bad seed. Of course, we need not be healed of the good seeds, such as positive reinforcement and parental grace. But all of us, like fertile seedbeds, have received mutated seeds that have produced distorted and defective fruit, which in turn, contain more seed which will be sown in our own future generations.

We are surrounded by such children as this little boy. Oh, they may not look like children to us as they walk about disguised as parents, teachers, waitresses, construction workers, lawyers, doctors, and the rest. But inside, where they really live, they are little children with heads hung low, afraid to look us in the eye, wondering what we will think of them. They wonder whether we see them hiding in grown-up bodies, playing dress-up in Mommy and Daddy's clothing.

Before we get too indignant and upset about the teacher in this event, we have to remember that her response was probably the fruit of seed in her own life as well. She was living out of whatever was filling her heart. Jesus said, "Whatever is in your heart determines what you say" (Lk. 6:45 NLT). Shameful seeds were probably planted in this teacher's heart somewhere along the line, and she was merely producing the fruit of those seeds. She, as a wounded child, then physically grew into an adult, but inside there was still a child afraid that her concert would go awry if a careless little crooner was allowed to sing. She couldn't risk the disapproval of parents and peers present there. It makes me wonder where that seed of shame was planted in her life. The possibilities are endless, but to be sure, her wounding of the little boy in her music class was the fruit of the seed planted in her own life.

Though there are many sources of programming during our early years, home and family are the primary seedbed that determines what kind of fruit we will produce the rest of our lives. They are like a mirror affecting how we see ourselves, a skylight affecting how we see God, a window affecting how we see other people, and a door affecting how we see the rest of the world.[1]

No, we aren't trying to excuse everyone's sin and hurtful behavior, but we need to look beyond the obvious and allow our hearts to be filled with understanding and compassion to see the other wounded children around us.

When this little boy was stifled, the seed of a lie was planted in his heart. It was a lie that said something like, "You're no good," or "You're an embarrassment," or any number of other variations. I have used this true account during some of our equipping events and have been amazed at how many times it has elicited tears from the class as they recall similar events in their own lives. I have seen a few hang their heads just like the little boy as they remember a bad oral reading experience in school, or a parent or older sibling who ridiculed them.

Living in God's Face

Beloved, the Lord has passion for our little faces. We were created to live in His presence, literally His face,[2] with nothing between our face and His. Seeing our faces is the priority of His affection and purpose in us. The grown-up in us wants to convince us that God's purpose is some ponderous and important ministry where we can lose ourselves in what we do. But in truth, our greatest purpose is simply to be with Him...to live in His

---

1. David Seamands, *Healing Grace* (Indianapolis, IN: Light and Life Communication, 2002), pp. 47-52.

2. The Hebrew words for *face* and *presence* are the same, *Paniym*.

presence. I believe that this is why the first commandment God gave to Israel was, "You shall have no other god, or anything else for that matter, between your face and Mine" (literal paraphrase of Ex. 20:3). If we could really understand this first commandment, the others might be a little easier to follow.

Somewhere along the line, we were wounded and our attention shifted away from the presence or face of God and onto our hurts. We have turned away from the living God and serve lesser gods like fear and shame and consequently are stuck in time. When anger arises within us at the slightest circumstance, it is the anger and insecurity of a wounded little child who is still alive in us and who is separated from the face of God.

I think again of the little boy in singing class whose attention was turned toward himself to avoid further wounding. His ability to receive love from a fathering God was skewed because of what one insecure adult did to him. Little children believe what grown-ups say as gospel…grown-ups are grown-ups and surely they would not lie to us. If they say we are lousy, then it must be so.[3] Grown-ups are themselves wounded children with a need to get back to the face of the One who created them.

The Wounded Children Among Us

In heart-healing sessions I've seen a wounded and sad little girl of 12 who was turned away from the church door because of the side of the tracks she lived on, who was now dressed as a 70-year-old grandmother trying to find her place in God. I've seen a young man of 15 who could never do anything good enough for his father and was now wearing an expensive suit living in terror of making mistakes while he ran a large corporation. There are many people of all ages wearing many disguises, yet they all are children.

I recall ministering to a young man who in his adult life struggled to find personal approval and tended to be a loner keeping himself from deep and accountable relationships. When we

---

3.   David Seamands, *Healing Grace* (Indianapolis, IN: Light and Life Communication, 2002).

prayed together, we found an 11-year-old boy inside who had been given a trumpet solo to play and made a few mistakes. When the concert was over, the young trumpeter was found backstage by his father. The little boy expected his dad would be thrilled that he had performed a solo. Instead, his father, a public figure said, "Well boy, you blew it." Needless to say, he was crushed, and a seed was planted that day that brought a harvest of shame in his future. His dad's cruel and self-focused remarks planted a lie in his son's heart that drove him to perform in isolation and never feel safe in a father's love.

What are we to do with all the wounded children around us? It is interesting to note that the children we have mentioned are believers and serve the Lord the best way they know how. Their spiritual condition is not the issue. The issue is the seed-lies that were planted and carried around, affecting their lives and relationships on every level with God and man alike. We might add that each one encountered the presence of the living God and found truth, order, and peace in their lives.

Wounded children surround us. We cover them up and ignore them, but they are there. Some of them are *us*. The Lord is not willing to leave any children alone in their pain but longs to bring us into His presence so that we may experience ultimate healing. Beloved, as our compassionate Father saw us during those evil seeding events, He was not content to stand by and allow them to happen, but began to lead us gently toward His healing heart. On the day of our wounding, He was already leading us to the day of healing in His presence. Beloved, this is the day!

An Invitation of Healing

The little boy in the singing class was invited back to that place of trauma and shame, a scene now filled with the healing presence of God. The place of pain became holy ground where the Lord took up the baton and conducted, while the little boy sang joyfully into the smiling face of the King of kings. Beloved, such an invitation awaits all of us as children. God is a compassionate and gracious God who speaks to the little children in us, inviting us to healing in His embrace.

We are surrounded by suffering children—children who need Jesus. When I read *"Suffer the little children to come unto Me,"* I can see Jesus delighting in all the little faces. Can you hear Him say, "Bring them to Me…bring the little faces to Me"? Dear one, He is looking for your face. He is inviting that little wounded one in you into His presence to wipe away your tears and tell you the truth about yourself.

Whatever has distracted your face from God's, whatever obstacle has been placed in your life, it can be removed in Christ. "All of us like sheep have gone astray, each of us has turned to his own way; but the Lord has caused the iniquity of us all to fall on Him" (Is. 53:6). He Himself is our peace—He is the One who longs to be gracious to us and to lavish His presence and compassion upon us, to bring us to truth and order and peace. He has seen us and now extends His open arms to invite us to healing saying, " 'I have seen…I will heal…I will lead…and comfort…creating the praise of the lips. Peace, peace to him who is far and to him who is near,' says the Lord, 'and I will heal him' " (Is. 57:18-19).

CHAPTER TWO

A FULLER GOSPEL

When the Lord your God brings you into the land where you are entering to possess it... (Deuteronomy 7:1).

At no other time does our relationship with God show up more accurately than on Monday morning. Most of us attend Sunday morning services filled with beautiful music that prepares the way for some kind of thought-provoking teaching. And all of it transpires in the ambiance of spiritual brothers and sisters who smile at us in the warmth and generosity of Christian concern and comfort. As the service concludes, we are sure that we have heard or felt something from God that day, and we believe we are inoculated for the rest of the week against the disease of despair.

However, the peace that seems to blanket us in the presence of God already begins to wane with the final strains of music as we stroll out the door and get into our vehicle. A strange empty feeling follows us as we walk through the rest of the day and towards the events of the coming week. We don't think too much of it, though; this is the routine we have followed for years—Sunday after Sunday, meeting after meeting, Bible study after Bible study. But what is this emptiness we feel?

On Monday morning we awaken with the Novocain of religious ecstasy having worn off, and we face life feeling emotionally naked and alone. A helpless, pointless, numb feeling carries us through the days and events of our routine. Our lives seem to waver between terror and tedium as we walk through our days in a kind of emotional fog that never allows us to see or discern objectively. In one sense it feels like someone is riding on our backs and sinking his spurs into our skin in order to drive us by some kind of pain. We live fenced in by feelings we cannot explain and dare not discuss on Sunday, for to do so would be to incur the disdain of the righteous. Nothing is ever supposed to be wrong in our lives. We are Christians, after all!

Nevertheless, we wake up on Monday morning the same way that many do who do not call themselves Christians. This same reality surrounds those who don't go to church. They feel the same emptiness and controlling emotional spurs. They may find some solace in their work or in some kind of New Age spiritual transcendence, but they feel the same way on Monday that we do. They, as well as we, ask the same question: "Is this all there is?"

Many Christians are hounded by fear, rejection, worthlessness, shame, insecurity, defilement, hopelessness, or some combination of any or all of these. We may have a "saving knowledge" that we are bound for Heaven, but at the same time we live out a kind of emotional hell on earth. Many in the Body of Christ have yet to experience their "re-birthright" in Jesus Christ. Although we *should* be living in the power and purpose of God, we instead limp from one day to the next waiting to go to Heaven. However, this is *not* God's idea. This is *not* all there is to life on earth. Why do we live so far below our position in Christ? The truth is that while we may know the gospel, we have yet to *believe* it!

Longing for Love and Acceptance

There is a "fuller gospel" than the one we have believed. The real good news is that God desires to "bring us into" a life of abundance in Christ. Jesus told us that He came so you and I "may have life, and have it abundantly" (Jn. 10:10b). He wants to take us beyond our emotional pain and limping limitations to a place characterized by the unconditional love and acceptance that we all long for and seldom realize. It is a place of peace and rest from the torment of satanically inspired lies that rob us of intimacy with God.

The greatest emotional struggles we experience are the result of our lack of understanding the simple truth that by His grace, God "hath made us accepted in the beloved [Jesus Christ]" (Eph. 1:6 KJV). This simple understanding could eliminate all emotional pain we suffer. The one thing that we all are looking for is a Father who will never abandon us or leave us alone. Thus the presence of God is the source of all healing. It is really what we all long for.

The apostle Paul understood how gloriously God met this most basic need of all people. Listen to his ecstatic praise in his letter to the Ephesians.

> *Blessed be the God and Father of our Lord Jesus Christ, who hath blessed us with all spiritual blessings in heavenly places in Christ: according as He hath* **chosen** *us in Him before the foundation of the world, that we should be holy and without blame before Him in love: having predestinated us unto the* **adoption** *of children by Jesus Christ to Himself, according to the good pleasure of His will, to the praise of the glory of His grace, wherein He hath made us* **accepted** *in the beloved* (Ephesians 1:3-6 KJV, emphasis added).

Look at the key words in these verses. We are *chosen* and *loved* or *accepted* by God's will. That is the very description of the term *adoption* that Paul uses so many times throughout the Epistles. When a couple adopts a baby, they *choose* a child to *love*. Likewise, God chooses us. However, God does not go through an orphanage with a list of expectations and descriptions looking for perfect children. Rather, God picks us up as we lay in our dirty diapers with the sole intention of loving us, and He will never put us down again! He has chosen us and loved us "to the praise of the glory of His grace"! God has *chosen* us and *loved* us simply because He desires to do so. How much of our pain could be alleviated—how many of our wounds healed—if we could truly experience and believe this astounding and irrational love of God?

God has always desired to express His love for man. In the Torah, God moved the nation of Israel toward a "homeland" where His love and acceptance would be the rule of life. It was the thought of this homeland that captivated the life of Abraham, who "by faith…lived as an alien in the land of promise, as in a foreign land, dwelling in tents with Isaac and Jacob, fellow heirs of the same promise; for he was looking for the city which has foundations, whose architect and builder is God" (Heb. 11:9-10). God promised Abraham a home—an inheritance that God would secure by His own faithfulness (see Gen. 15)—and the only requirement was that Abraham would trust God to do it. We today have entered into the same promises God made to Abraham by the blood of Christ. And God also is moving us toward this place that feels like home, or at least feels like the way home should feel.

Dr. Larry Crabb, author of *Effective Biblical Counseling*, refers to these two primary needs of love and acceptance as the needs for "security" and "significance." These became needs as a result of our broken relationship with God. Dr. Crabb says,

> I believe that at the fall Adam and Eve were both significant and secure. From the moment of their creation their needs were fully met in a relationship with God unmarred by sin. Significance and security were attributes of qualities already resident in their personalities, so they never gave them a second thought. When sin ended their innocence and broke their relationship with God, what formerly were attributes became needs.[1]

We are "secure" in the *love* of God and "significant" in that God has *chosen* us. There can be no higher significance than to be chosen by the One who created us. Apart from our understanding that we are chosen or accepted by God, we will try all manner of things to achieve acceptability, most of which will end up wounding us further. On the other hand, out of the love and acceptance of God comes all that we could ever want or need for a whole and meaningful life. And that is where God is taking us—that is what He desires to "bring us into."

---

1.   Dr. Larry Crabb, *Effective Biblical Counseling* (Grand Rapids, MI: Zondervan Publishing House, 1977), p. 61.

What Life Was Meant to Be

As we read the biblical narrative of creation, we see that God's design for us was simple (see Gen. 1:27-28; 2:7-8,15). God's desire was communion with man, and all of man's needs would be met entirely in his communion with God. For a time, man lived in the pure and unadulterated truth of God's love and acceptance and enjoyed emotional wholeness. There was no fear, no rejection, no unworthiness—only total trust in an atmosphere of truth and purposeful intimacy. This was what God meant life to be for all of us. Alas, man succumbed to the lies of the serpent and became separated from God in sin. (We will discuss this more fully in the next chapter.)

In Deuteronomy 7:7 Moses tells Israel that "the Lord did not set His love on you nor choose you because you were more in number than any of the peoples, for you were the fewest of all peoples." In other words, God did not offer them love and acceptance because of anything they did or deserved, but simply out of His own nature and desire for intimate fellowship. The place into which God was leading Israel in Deuteronomy chapter 7 was an Old Testament example of the place where God now is leading those who are in Christ.

The "land" that is spoken of in Deuteronomy 7 typifies a place of intimate communion between God and His people where all that was lost in Eden would be restored. There would be no more fear or separation from God, and every facet of man's life would be wrapped up and lived in the presence of God. God in Christ has brought us into this place, though few have entered into it fully.

Out of God's love and acceptance for His people Israel flowed all that was necessary for their life and prosperity. God brought them into a land of "cities which you did not build, and houses full of all good things which you did not fill, and hewn cisterns which you did not dig," and "vineyards and olive trees which you did not plant..." (Deut. 6:10b-11). In other words, they were to experience the "riches of His grace" just as Paul mentioned in Ephesians 1:7. All that the Israelites would have or achieve would be a by-product of the grace of a loving Father and the intimacy He restored.

The Bible describes this "grace-land" in several ways. Let's look briefly at a few of these riches, for each points to something that we should be experiencing today as children of God in Christ Jesus.

Rest and Peace

It was to be a land "flowing with milk and honey" (Deut. 6:3b). When our daughters were babies and refused to fall asleep, my wife used an Old World sedative that worked every time. As the girls lay fidgeting in their beds, Carol would heat up some milk and add some honey to it. After our daughters took a few sips of nature's sleeping potion, they would soon drift off to a sweet slumber. It was a sure way to still even the greatest up-heaval of the day. The taste of milk and honey meant love to our children. I wish sometimes that I could recapture but a snapshot of that restful sleep that used to come across the faces of our lit-tle ones as they lay in bed. When I think of a "land flowing with milk and honey," I envision a place of rest and peace. This rest and peace are the result of dwelling in God's love and acceptance.

Note that the Bible says it was a land "flowing" with milk and honey. It was not just trickling; it was flowing. There was no scarcity of supply—no fear that anyone would lack provision. This new homeland was the place where fear and want would be totally dispatched in favor of God's abundance.

Today Christ has *become* our peace (see Eph. 2:14). But how many of us really live in the peace and rest that Christ has provided at the cost of His own blood? Many fidget and squirm in the lap of God. Many could use a sip of the real milk and honey of Christ's peace. If we are not experiencing that peace in our lives, God wants to bring us into a new place of understand-ing of the truth that brings peace.

Communion With God

The land into which Israel was being led was a place of communion with God—a place of intimate fellowship where

God would be involved and acknowledged in every phase of life. God Himself told the nation many times of His desire to enjoy intimate communion with them.

> *I will give to you and to your descendants after you, the land of your sojournings, all the land of Canaan, for an everlasting possession; and I will be their God* (Genesis 17:8).

> *I will also walk among you and be your God, and you shall be My people* (Leviticus 26:12).

> *Let them construct a sanctuary for Me, that I may dwell among them* (Exodus 25:8).

> *I will dwell among the sons of Israel and will be their God* (Exodus 29:45).

Communion was foremost in God's heart as He prepared the nation of Israel to cross over into the land of grace. Intimate communion is God's plan for us as well. In Christ, God brought all mankind back into this relationship of intimate communion— a purposeful intimacy where all that man was and all that he did flowed from his oneness with God. Jesus said, "If anyone loves Me, he will keep My word; and My Father will love him, and We will come to him and make Our abode [have communion] with him" (Jn. 14:23). In other words, obedience and purpose flow out of our intimacy with God. It is God's desire that we experience His presence and involvement in every facet of our lives. All that God has done for us in Christ leads to this intimate relationship.

Purpose and Worth

God also intended the nation of Israel to derive their purpose and worth from their unique relationship with Him. In fact, it was their relationship with God that set them apart from all other people on earth. Moses says, "For how then can it be known that I have found favor in Your sight, I and Your people? Is it not by Your going with us, so that we, I and Your people, may be distinguished from all the other people who are upon the face of the earth?" (Ex. 33:16) It was God's "going with" Israel—His presence among them—that gave them their "distinguishing" purpose and worth. So it is for us who are in Christ. It is our relationship with Christ that distinguishes us from all others. It is our position in Christ that determines our worth and purpose.

We live in a time when people wander from place to place searching for purpose and meaning in their lives. Recently I was in the great city of London, England. One evening I decided to set out on my own to walk a bit in the streets and look at the people. As I walked, I encountered people from many nations speaking several languages. They all were so different, yet they all were the same. They all had a look of aimlessness. They talked, shopped, and ate as if waiting for something to happen. They were going nowhere, and I'm sure that most arrived at that destination. As I looked into their eyes, I saw that life seemed to be a meaningless syncopation of events and purposeless wanderings for them.

The world assigns us our worth based on how much money we make or the titles and influence we hold, but our worth cannot be measured in dollars. Our true purpose and worth stem from our relationship with God. We are what we are by the grace of God. Those in Christ exist for the purpose of fellowship with God, giving Him glory through their lives. While the world works to *gain* acceptance, those in Christ work *because* of their acceptance in Christ.

God's plan for us is peace, rest, communion, purpose, and worth, and we obtain all of these "in Christ."

Taking Us Into the Land

God has already prepared for us a place of wholeness where we have been chosen and loved in Christ. All of the things we've discussed and much more are ours in Christ. He has become our inheritance. Unfortunately, many of us never experience the rest, peace, communion, purpose, and worth that are ours in Christ. We are tormented by negative emotions of fear, shame, and all the rest. However, in Christ we are chosen and loved, and it is out of this reality that our emotions are healed.

The presence of God demonstrates His healing power and reassurance of His love.

- When we feel fear...   Christ is with us.
- When we feel rejected...   Christ accepts us.
- When we feel worthless...   Christ approves us.
- When we feel shame...   Christ covers us.
- When we feel insecure...   Christ surrounds us.
- When we feel defiled...   Christ restores us.
- When we feel hopeless...   Christ becomes our living hope.

We must realize that there is an active and deliberate plan devised to keep us from experiencing all of these benefits in Christ. Our common enemy cannot do anything to affect our salvation through Christ, but he will do his best to keep us from entering the rest and communion that are ours by Christ's own blood. There are great riches for us—a table of blessings to which we have been called. It is a table of chosenness and love under the grace of a loving Father.

So let us know, let us press on to know the Lord. His going forth is as certain as the dawn; and He will come to us like the rain, like the spring rain watering the earth (Hosea 6:3).

CHAPTER THREE

LIVING THE LIES THAT BIND

...and clears away many nations before you, the Hittites and the Girgashites and the Amorites and the Canaanites and the Perizzites and the Hivites and the Jebusites, seven nations greater and stronger than you (Deuteronomy 7:1).

One afternoon my wife, Carol, and I were ministering to a couple in our congregation. Throughout the ministry session, I saw Carol crying several times. I thought, *Wow. She is really into this session—really pouring herself out to the Lord for this couple.* But when the ministry time was over and we were leaving, the tears didn't stop. In fact, they intensified as we got in the car. It was pretty obvious, even to me, that something was happening inside Carol's heart. I didn't know what, though, so I asked her.

She replied that during the session when I read the verses from Psalm 139, "For You formed my inward parts; You wove me in my mother's womb. I will give thanks to You, for I am fearfully and wonderfully made; wonderful are Your works, and my soul knows it very well" (Ps. 139:13-14), the words triggered something in her. She didn't believe she was very wonderfully made. In fact, she saw herself as never able to do anything well. In short, she believed a lie.

When we arrived home, we prayed that the Lord would reveal the source of this lie to her. In response, the Lord escorted Carol to a memory picture[1] of her third-grade classroom. One day a little girl who was partially blind came into the class, and

---

1. "Memory picture" is a term used by Theophostic Ministry. See *Beyond Tolerable Recovery*, Edward M. Smith, page 41. Also see comments on "reframing" memories from *Inner Healing* by Mike Flynn and Doug Gregg, pages 82-83.

Carol's teacher asked her to look after the new student. Needless to say, Carol felt pretty special about her assignment. It was a gesture of approval from her teacher, but it soon came crashing down—along with her confidence.

Sometime after lunch, Carol's teacher came to her and said, "I think we'd better let someone else help this little girl." My wife did not hear or remember any reason why she should not continue to help this little girl. All she heard was that she was not able to do it to suit the teacher. She was devastated—humiliated. There was this picture of Carol as a little third-grade child sadly slumped over her desk coloring in a book, alone. What she felt was that she was not good enough to take care of the new girl— that there must have been something wrong with her. Because of this and other similar experiences, Carol grew up with a feeling of inadequacy. She lacked the confidence needed in order to follow through with good ideas. She heard an inner voice telling her, "You can't do this" or "You're not good enough for that."

When we asked the Lord to reveal to her the truth as opposed to the lie, Carol saw our own daughter, Coco, sitting at a desk instead of her. (Carol is a schoolteacher and has had both of her daughters in class, so this scene was not a stretch.) As we prayed, the presence of the Lord seemed to pour into the memory picture and a question arose from the midst of the scene. The Lord asked Carol, "How do you feel about this little girl?" Carol said, "I love her; I delight in her." The Lord responded, "And I delight in you!" Just then the feeling of worthlessness dissipated. Carol knew at last from the heart of God how He felt about her. And she believed it.

In the following months, Carol began to pursue the formation of a new drama department at the Christian school where she teaches—something she could never have done before because of a lack of confidence. The Lord led her to put on a production of "The Miracle Worker" throughout which she wove the words of Psalm 139 and the truth that God had brought her out of the darkness and into the light—that she was wonderfully made by the hand of God. Hundreds of people were privileged to see the result of that healing truth as we wept at the healing grace of God.

This story demonstrates the usual course that the ministry of inner healing takes. When we learn the truth, it overcomes the lies we believe about God and ourselves, and restores us to intimacy with God. Although Carol is obviously a talented and anointed woman, she believed and lived under the power of the lie that she could never do anything good enough. The comments and disapproval of her third-grade teacher eroded her confidence. Carol, like many of us, was living a lie—a lie that denies the truth about us and about the love and acceptance that is ours in Christ. Her healing, and ours, comes as we experience the truth of who we are in Christ.

The Truth About Truth

In order to uncover the lies that bind us, we first need to know about truth. In order to receive truth and healing for our emotional wounds, we must understand what the truth is. I don't want to engage in philosophical questions about the nature of truth, although it can be a fascinating discussion. Instead, I want to state what truth is in its biblical definition.

Truth Is What Is True

Simply put, truth is what is real, and what is real is what comes from God. The Hebrew word for truth is *émet*, which comes from the same word that we know as *amen. Émet* refers to something that is true in its essence; it is faithful, real, dependable, and powerful. When we hear something that registers with us as trustworthy, we say "Amen!" The New Testament word is *alethia*, which again refers to something that is true or real versus what is false. Conversely, what is untrue is also unfaithful, unreal, undependable, and powerless—unless we empower it by believing it.

Another way to describe truth is to say that truth, insofar as God is concerned, is that which is whole or in order. When God speaks truth, the result is order. He spoke a word, and worlds came into being. Psalm 33:6 says that He spoke the heavens into existence. Whatever God speaks brings order and the resulting peace or wholeness. This is the Hebrew concept of *shalom*, which is a state of wholeness or integrity. Christ was *shalom* incarnate bringing truth, order, and peace to the earth. When the angels announced the birth to the shepherds, they announced that peace was "on earth"; they were proclaiming that order was being restored. The sequence then is truth, which restores order, which then results in peace with God. This is the same process that brings wholeness and peace in our individual lives. We must be put back in order to find emotional wholeness. And we must hear the truth if we are to be put back in order.

The opposite is also true. That which is untrue is out of order. When people wound us in some way, they have in effect spoken or done something that is against the order or the truth of God. They leave us out of order and without peace. When children hear that they are lazy or stupid or perhaps suffer the pain of sexual abuse, they believe something that is not true, and as a result they order their lives around lies. The truth is that they are precious creations of God, but the lies they believe as a result of wounding leave them "out of order" and living under feelings of worthlessness or shame, which limit and control their lives.

When I was a child, we used to build "houses" with dominos or cards. But if just one of those dominos or cards was taken away, the whole structure would collapse. It is the same with truth. If something is untrue in the slightest way, the whole thing collapses in untruth. It takes only a little lie to cause a life to come crashing to the ground.

On the other hand, whatever God says is entirely true; it is in order. His Word is true; therefore, it has true power and effect. God speaks something, and because He is the ultimate Truth, whatever He says becomes true as well. God spoke the world into existence. "Then God said, 'Let there be light'; and there was light" (Gen. 1:3). The universe is ordered through God's word. What is not based on God's truth is out of order. Healing comes as we hear and experience the truth of God, which restores God's order in us. When we receive truth, our beliefs are reordered and, with them, our emotions.

Christ Is the Truth

Jesus Christ was Himself the very incarnation of the truth of God. Jesus said, "I am the way, and the truth, and the life; no one comes to the Father but through Me" (Jn. 14:6). The Gospel of John says that Jesus was "full of grace and truth" and that Jesus has "explained" or demonstrated the truth about God's intention toward man.

> *And the Word became flesh, and dwelt among us, and we saw His glory, glory as of the only begotten from the Father, **full of grace and truth**. John testified about Him and cried out, saying, "This was He of whom I said, 'He who comes after me has a higher rank than I, for He existed before me.'" For of His fullness we have all received, and grace upon grace. For the Law was given through Moses; grace and truth were realized through Jesus Christ. No one has seen God at any time; the only begotten God who is in the bosom of the Father, He has explained Him* (John 1:14-18, emphasis added).

Jesus is the true expression of all that is God. He is the "exact representation" of God's heart toward us in that He came to reconcile and restore us to God (see Heb. 1:3). Truth is not a collection of facts no matter how well supported and obvious. Rather, truth is personified in Jesus Christ. So then, we know if something is true by whether or not it sounds like Jesus. (We will discuss more about the sound of truth in a later chapter.)

The Origin of Lies

Just as truth has a source—God—so do the lies we believe have an original source. Jesus calls this source the "father of lies" and said that he was that way from the very beginning (see Jn. 8:44). The lies and deception that we believe and live under are the product of a deliberate and diabolical plan to keep us separated from God. Into the Garden slithered the source and inspiration of all lies in the form of a serpent.

Now the serpent was more crafty than any beast of the field which the Lord God had made. And he said to the woman, "Indeed, has God said, 'You shall not eat from any tree of the garden'?" The woman said to the serpent, "From the fruit of the trees of the garden we may eat; but from the fruit of the tree which is in the middle of the garden, God has said, 'You shall not eat from it or touch it, or you will die.'" The serpent said to the woman, "You surely will not die! For God knows that in the day you eat from it your eyes will be opened, and you will be like God, knowing good and evil" (Genesis 3:1-5).

Satan's plan was to disrupt the union between God and man, to call God's unconditional love and acceptance into question, and to throw a monkey wrench between our face and His. Satan brought disorder into the world by asking, in effect, "Did God really say that you couldn't eat from this tree?" He was implying that God was somehow less loving than man might have believed. How could a loving God deny us anything? Then he added, "God knows that when you eat this fruit you will become like Him, knowing good and evil." Satan implied that God was holding out on man—that man could better serve his own purpose instead of God's. It is the grandfather of all life-sapping lies: "You can be like God…." For the first time, man was presented with the idea that he could live separated from God. The result was tragic.

When man believed the lie and ate from the tree of the knowledge of good and evil, his eyes were opened and he was separated from the life of God, the blessing of God, the purpose of God, and communion with God. Sin entered the world, leaving man hiding behind his man-made apron of fig leaves. But God, who is rich in mercy, came looking for man: "Adam, where are you?" Obviously God knew what man had done, but both then and now, God is more concerned with where we are than what we've done, and He calls us back to intimacy.

In the wake of man's separation from God, all that he enjoyed as part of the intimate fellowship with God was subverted by opposites. Unconditional love and acceptance were replaced by fear and shame. Open and intimate fellowship with God gave way to hiding behind fig leaves and bushes. This is not God's plan or desire for any of us.

There is a host of lies that rob us of intimacy with God and cause us to live in our own strength separate from God. Whereas, if we want to live in grace and emotional wholeness, we must uncover the lies we believe and subject them to the truth of God. The path the Israelites took to enter the Promised Land gives us some clues to these lies.

Greater and Stronger Influences

As Israel was about to cross into the inheritance of God, Moses warned them that they would encounter seven nations that were "greater and stronger" than they (see Deut. 7:1). These influences would be obstacles to the enjoyment of the kind of abundance and intimacy with God that He intended. The following lists some of the negative emotions these ungodly nations suggest.

Hittites:	*Fear*
Girgashites:	*Rejection*
Amorites:	*Worthlessness*
Canaanites:	*Shame*
Perizzites:	*Insecurity*
Hivites:	*Defilement*
Jebusites:	*Hopelessness*

The names of each of these pagan nations suggest a strong influence that inhabited the land of grace and abundance into which God was bringing His people Israel.[2] The negative emotional influences that these names suggest still inhabit the abundant life that you and I were promised. Jesus said, "I came that they may have life, and have it abundantly" (Jn. 10:10b). He was

---

2.   Compare these various influences with the categories of lies listed in *Beyond Tolerable Recovery*, pages 86-89. Also see *Deep Wounds, Deep Healing* by Charles H. Kraft, pages 183-188; and Healing of Memories by David A. Seamands, page 144.

comparing the kind of life He came to bring, with the kind of life inspired by the thief who comes to steal, kill, and destroy us. The devil is the thief, and he is the father of lies (see Jn. 8:44, 10:10a). He inspires fear, rejection, shame, and all the rest. On the other hand, the kind of life Jesus meant for us is not one controlled by lies, nagging fears, and limiting thoughts, but one of wholeness. This whole life is one that is lived in the understanding that we are loved and chosen by God in Christ Jesus.

How is it, you may ask, that a Christian can be so controlled by these influences? Aren't we saved and bought by the blood of Christ? The answer is yes. Of course we are. But the battle we're talking about here has nothing to do with our salvation, which is a matter of spirit. The battleground is in our minds, which remain under the influence of the world and are in the process of being transformed. From that old self, from that old mind-set, we have heard and believed lies.

> *Do not lie to one another, since you laid aside the old self with its evil practices, and have put on the new self who is being renewed to a true knowledge according to the image of the One who created him* (Colossians 3:9-10).

Here Paul is telling us that there is an old "self" or mind that is being renewed or renovated so that it agrees with the salvation we have received in our spirits. However, this old self or mind continues to reflect our old sinful and carnal nature; in addition, it carries with it the wounds and memories from the past along with the lies that provide them the soil to live in. The lies that were planted in our past still bear fruit in the present.

The process that uncovers these lies and allows us an unobstructed view of God is what we refer to as inner healing. Paul, dealing with the believers in Rome, describes the process of rooting out the lies of the world as "renewing the mind."

> *And do not be conformed to this world, but be transformed by the renewing of your mind, so that you may*

prove what the will of God is, that which is good and acceptable and perfect (Romans 12:2).

What is untrue has no power unless we believe it. And if we experience it enough, we may come to believe even a greater lie. Jesus said that even the very elect, those close to God, can be deceived (see Mk. 13:22). Of course, in that passage Jesus was speaking of false messiahs, but the principle is the same for any other lie. In the opening story about Carol, it was not true that she was unacceptable or unlovable, but she had heard and experienced disapproval from a respected adult teacher and came to believe it. (To be sure, she had other similar memories, but the Lord chose that particular one to reveal His heart to Carol.) Nevertheless, what was totally false and baseless gained power over Carol's life. Until she learned the truth, her life was bound by a lie.

Everything we believe is not necessarily true. We come to believe something by our experience or perhaps through the environment in which we grew up. At the same time, God's love for us and His desire to see us healed and in fellowship with Him are true. Our belief in something does not make it true—rather it is true so we can believe it!

The traveling companion of truth is peace. As we mentioned earlier, peace, or *shalom* in Hebrew, refers to a state of wholeness. The relationship between truth and peace is seen throughout the Scriptures. Truth brings healing, as the Lord spoke through the prophet Jeremiah in referring to His desire to restore the lost nation of Israel: "Behold, I will bring to it health and healing, and I will heal them; and I will reveal to them an abundance of peace and truth" (Jer. 33:6). *Truth brings order, and order brings peace or wholeness.*

The Healing Truth

The truest thing in the universe is that God loves us. The Scriptures say, "God is love" (1 Jn. 4:8b). The truth of God's love was nailed to the cross and put on display for the world to see. His love is *real*. This is the glory of God, who made us pure by

His own blood and enabled us to return to fellowship with the Father. Unfortunately, even though we are saved and reunited with God in spirit, our minds are still caught in the thorns of Eden's curse. It is because we as Christians do not understand who we are and what Christ has done for us—the truth—that we still experience fear, rejection, worthlessness, shame, powerlessness, and hopelessness. God's desire is to bring us the truth to heal our wounded and distorted emotions.

Actually, the truth that brings us healing is not merely a correction of inadequate data; the Truth is the presence and voice of Jesus Christ Himself. While separation from God is the source of all wounds and emotional dysfunction, our restoration to intimacy in His presence then becomes the source of our healing.

In the following chapters we will learn that Christ, the harbinger of God's love and acceptance, destroys each of the lies we believe about God and ourselves. God desires to bring us into the truth and peace within intimate fellowship with Himself. We serve a healing and restoring God who is not content to leave us in our emotional pain, but who leads us to Himself and the restoration of our fellowship with Him.

Now let me close with this prophetic pronouncement: The Lord loves you and He intends to bring you to a new place of intimacy and healing in His presence. Oh, how the Lord longs to bring you into His presence and pour out His healing grace upon you. He will become your Teacher—the voice of truth in your heart that destroys all the false images and lies that have robbed you of His abundant life. The Lord Himself will lead you as He speaks to you. Listen and turn toward His voice.

Hear now the words of the prophet Isaiah:

But the Lord still waits for you to come to Him so He can show you His love and compassion. For the Lord is a faithful God. Blessed are those who wait for Him to help them. O people of Zion, who live in Jerusalem, you will weep no more. He will be gracious if you ask for help. He will respond instantly to the sound of your cries. Though the Lord gave you adversity for food and affliction for drink, He will still be with you to teach you. ***You will see your teacher with your own eyes, and you will hear a voice say, "This is the way; turn around and walk here."*** *Then you will destroy all your silver idols and gold images. You will throw them out like filthy rags. "Ugh!" you will say to them. "Be-gone!"* (Isaiah 30:18-22 NLT, emphasis added)

CHAPTER FOUR

EMOTIONAL ECHOES

Man is disturbed not by things, but by what he believes
about them.

—Epictetus, a Stoic philosopher of the first century

There is a sound I recall from my school days that still has
the power to make me cringe today. You remember it. The teacher
would be standing at the chalkboard writing and suddenly his or
her fingernail would scrape against the board. The result was a
kind of dry squealing sound that disrupted every nerve in your
body from the roots of your teeth to the curled toes on your feet.
What this small sound lacked in decibels it more than made up
for in its ability to immobilize everybody within earshot. You
may wince even now as the recollection of this sound overpow-
ers you. What you heard and felt in that classroom long ago
echoes in your mind today.

An echo is a voice or sound reflecting off some distant object. Think of being in a large canyon with a long distance across
the chasm. You shout, and a few seconds later your voice hits the
hard walls of the opposite side of the canyon and bounces back
to you. An echo also can be a voice that agrees with or reflects
another voice. For instance, we might "echo" someone's opinion.
The bottom line is that echoes sound the same across distance,
whether that distance is of time or space. The memory of that
sound of fingernails on a chalkboard is an echo reflecting off an
experience long ago.

There are other "sounds"—echoes of the past—that have the
ability to cause us to cringe in the present. These are emotional
echoes or associations that control us.[1] Just like that screeching

---

1.   "Emotional echo" is a term coined by Edward M. Smith in *Beyond Tol-
     erable Recovery*, page 39.

sound we remember from our school days, these "sounds" set off a response in us that causes us to recoil in fear, rejection, worthlessness, or some other strong negative emotion. We all experience these controlling emotional echoes to one degree or another. We encounter an emotional echo when an experience today reflects off of one that felt the same in the past, then bounces back to us with the same emotion of the original event. In other words, I feel now whatever I felt then.

All of us have experienced some kind of controlling emotional echo, whether it has been loud or barely audible. These echoes control us in the sense that they cause us to act in ways that the world would see as irrational or out of proportion. There may be times when the slightest provocation causes us to blow up in anger or shrink back in terror. We realize we are being controlled by these echoes when our emotional response is out of balance with what is happening around us. It is as if one sound is being created around us, but we hear something totally different from what everyone else does. Someone is playing a violin, and we are hearing an oboe. Remember, I am talking about Christians here—people bought by the blood of the Lamb of God and bound for glory. Whatever the cause, the resulting negative feelings seize control of us and rob us of the benefits of our life in Christ.

I remember once witnessing what seemed to be a ridiculous argument about a car. Two men had recently purchased similar cars, and one man remarked to the other that their cars were pretty much the same. The second man flew into an irrational tirade that the cars were not the same, that his car was a newer and better model than the other man's. You'd have thought that the first man had spit in the other's face. *Who cares what kind of car they had?* we might say to ourselves. However, this was about more than cars, you see. The enraged man stormed out the door, leaving the other man shrugging his shoulders wondering what had caused such a heated response.

Looking back now, it seemed as though the man who became angry believed he had to be right—he had to have something better. The casual comment his friend made regarding the car set in motion an echo from somewhere in his past that told him he had to be right or risk being somehow devalued as a person. The argument in the present was not about cars; it was about the man's self-worth—it was an emotional echo.

Something "greater and stronger" was controlling the man in the illustration. His response had little to do with a car. It was an echo—a tie to some other place in his life that felt like the present event. He was living in two places and two events at one time—the past and the present—and feeling the same about both. He had been threatened in the past and that emotion traveled into the present. One man was talking about cars and the other about life itself.

Feeling What We Believe

There is a relationship between what we *feel* and what we *believe*. Our emotions are not based on what is absolutely true, but what feels true to us. What we *feel* is the product of what we *believe*, and what we believe is a product of what we have *experienced*. The order is *experience, beliefs*, then *feelings*.[2]

For example, two men may be walking down the street and they encounter a big black dog, but based upon their own life experiences, they may feel entirely different about the dog. A big black dog may have bitten one of the men as a child while the other may have grown up in a family who owned a big black dog. One person will feel fear and the other joy at seeing the same big black dog under the same conditions at the same time. Nevertheless, what they experienced previously determines what they now believe. Both of them feel as they did earlier in their lives because they believe now what they believed then. So, as Epictetus the Stoic said, "Man is disturbed not by things, but by what he believes about them" (paraphrased).

In the course of everyday life, our minds pick up thousands of words and thoughts. Some of them stay with us while the rest

---

2.   For further study on the connection of emotions and beliefs see "Renewing Mind," *Rational Christian Thinking*, by Alice Petersen, Gary Sweeten, and Dorothy Faye Geverdt, pages 3:1 through 3:21. Also see chapter three of *Beyond Tolerable Recovery* by Edward Smith, pages 39-57.

fade away—they are deleted from our memory. The things that stick with us, however, usually are associated with some strong emotions of some kind, pleasant or not. These past emotions are the hard surfaces off of which our present emotions echo.

Those of us who are old enough will never forget where we were when we heard that President John F. Kennedy was shot. I was at Central Junior High School walking down a flight of stairs on my way to science class with Mrs. Oliver when a kid came running up the stairs to tell us what he had seen on TV.

I also can remember what I had for supper the day our daughter Amy was born. I had chili in the hospital cafeteria. It was lousy, but I remember it. The feeling I had about President Kennedy's assassination was of sorrow, and the emotion I experienced at my daughter's birth was joy. Both strongly resonate in my memory. I feel now what I felt then whenever those memories are triggered.

All in all, there are several distant surfaces off of which our emotions might be reflected—places where what we feel now is a reflection of what we felt then. Here are a few of them.

Distant Reflective Surfaces

Trauma, Joy

Have you ever been in a traffic accident? Perhaps there's a certain street that you used to drive down every day without any thought or remembrance. But one day while on that street, another car bumped into yours. You might, even now, still remember the time of day, what you were wearing, the name of the other driver, the color of the car that hit yours, or any number of other things. Not only that, but now each time you drive through that area your hands might tighten a little bit on the steering wheel and you may look around a little longer because of the trauma of the accident. Why does this happen? It's because your present thoughts and feelings are echoes of the previous trauma.

Our present emotions also can bounce off times of repeated abuse. Each wound or event gives opportunity for a lie to be recorded in our minds that plays back when we are reminded of the original event. It can be deliberate embarrassment, physical abuse, or sexual abuse. But when someone comes along who has a similar voice, dresses the same way, or appears in a similar situation, we may begin to feel the same kind of fear or nausea we felt in those times of abuse. The trigger to this echo can be just about anything—as long as it reminds us of what happened before. (There will be several examples of these kinds of abuse in the chapters ahead.)

Family Dysfunction

Those who grow up in dysfunctional families (and most families are dysfunctional in one way or another) may hear echoing voices from parents, teachers, or others telling us that we are not good enough. I have heard adults make such statements, reflecting the past, as, "You're just stupid," or "You will never be anything…." Believe it or not, these things may have been recorded decades earlier and subsequently become part of the operating system of the one who heard them. Each time that person faces a challenge or an opportunity, he or she hears these words bouncing off the hard wall of the distant past.

Sometimes family dysfunction may appear in the inability to show affection or love among family members. I can't tell you how many times I have heard someone say, "We just weren't a 'huggy' family…we knew that we were loved, but we didn't show it physically." Some of those whom we have heard say something like this struggle with feelings of worthlessness or insecurity today. There was a lie at work in that family that said love did not have to be demonstrated. That lie continues to echo today as they have grown up, gotten married, and had families, who also have trouble showing affection. Some end up with rebellious kids and have extramarital affairs.

Generational Sin

There are lies that grow on family trees as well. Today these might be referred to as generational sin. Here's a simple description of the concept of generational sin: If the parents plant poison ivy in the backyard, their children are going to itch. Parents set the tone in the family—they establish a family culture. Children naturally pick up what the parents demonstrate. Children often echo things that we don't want to hear. If Daddy treats Mommy with disdain and disrespect, then little Suzy may grow up looking for a husband to treat her the same way.

The Bible says that the sins committed in the family will come knocking on the door of subsequent generations. God told Moses and Israel not to give their children to the pagan influences and families around them. God said, "You shall not worship them or serve them; for I, the Lord your God, am a jealous God, visiting the iniquity of the fathers on the children, on the third and the fourth generations of those who hate Me" (Ex. 20:5). The "them" God is talking about are false gods and influences like fear, rejection, shame, and all the rest. Children live with the consequences of their parents' choices, not necessarily the guilt of them. In fact, they have a better-than-even chance of doing whatever it was that they saw their parents doing. If the parents serve those false gods and influences, then the children will as well.

Culture

Our feelings today—what we think of and how we relate to the world around us—may spring from the culture in which we were raised. There may be echoes of racial prejudice, gender bias, religious self-righteousness, or any manner of other such fruit growing out of a culture. For example, a young girl may grow up in a culture that tells her she is inferior and only good for having babies. She will be discouraged from going to school and developing her own abilities and talents. In another instance, one person may look down on another simply because of the individual's mode of dress or religious appearance.

I must include the church as a source of cultural emotional echoes. I suspect there is a lot of guilt and fear in the pews of the church. The place that ought to be the fountain of grace has often been the source of wounding and shame.

Sin Not Confessed

Some emotional echoes may be the result of sin that has not been dealt with. Many times we have ministered to people who have such a nagging sense of guilt or shame that they just can't move on with their lives. The problem may be that they never really confessed a sin in the past. In such cases the issue is resolved simply by confessing and then receiving grace and forgiveness in the presence of God.

Most likely there are other origins for the emotional echoes we hear in our present lives. But regardless of the source—the distant reflection point of the emotional echo—we must find a way to silence them…to delete or erase the lies upon which they resonate.

Silencing the Echoes

God's best is not for us to live under the power of the toxic tapes that play in our emotions today. Just as God showed Moses and the nation of Israel a way to silence the negative influences that threatened to control their lives, He has also promised to deliver these influences into our hands for us to destroy. In the next few chapters we will spend time locating the lies off of which our current emotions echo and silence them by acknowledging and declaring the truth of God.

The Spirit of God hears each emotional reflection in your heart and is even now beginning to identify them to you. These are the places where you feel afraid, shameful, or unsafe. They are the reasons you become angry at the slightest provocation or depressed at every turn. I pray that the Lord will open the eyes of your heart to see His heart and experience His healing, that you might be released from those hurtful echoes from the past.

I pray that the eyes of your heart may be enlightened, so that you will know what is the hope of His calling, what are the riches of the glory of His inheritance in the saints, and what is the surpassing greatness of His power toward us who believe. These are in accordance with the working of the strength of His might which He brought about in Christ, when He raised Him from the dead and seated Him at His right hand in the heavenly places, far above all rule and authority and power and dominion, and every name that is named, not only in this age but also in the one to come. And He put all things in subjection under His feet, and gave Him as head over all things to the church, which is His body, the fullness of Him who fills all in all (Ephesians 1:18-23).

CHAPTER FIVE

TEARING DOWN ALTARS

All of us want to find a place of greater peace and intimacy with our Creator—to get back into His face. We all want to dwell in His presence, to hear His voice clearly. Sometimes, instead of enjoying that peace, we are bombarded by nagging thoughts and inner voices vying for our attention and robbing us of peace and intimacy with God. These thoughts and voices are the things wired into us; they're our software. We cannot help but hear those voices and feel those emotions that control us, any more than we can help breathing in and out. The folks around us don't see what we see or feel what we feel. They have their own software problems to deal with. But there is help and healing for the influences that bind and control us. Now is the time to take out the garbage that has invaded our peace.

God has given us His Word to show us how to dismantle those influences and uncover the lies that bind us, so that we can live close to Him. He told Israel in Deuteronomy chapter 7 that He would deliver those seven nations—those influences—to them and give them an opportunity to destroy those nations. In Deuteronomy chapter 7, Yaweh proclaims His election of the nation of Israel as His own people based on a covenant of grace and guaranteed by His faithfulness. While this chapter concerns the election of Israel as the chosen people of God, it also suggests a basic statement. Yaweh is trying to take His people somewhere, but there are influences and obstacles in the way that must be removed. He gives His people steps to entering fully into the abundant life He has prepared for them and us.

Like the Israelites, we too can destroy those influences in our lives and live free from them. In this chapter, we will focus on uncovering the simple process by which the Lord allows us to find freedom and healing in His presence.

Instruction for Destruction

As Moses and Israel prepared to cross into the place of peace and abundance that God had prepared for them, God gave them specific instructions on how to eliminate the influences that would keep them from enjoying the peace and rest He had provided for them. These nations represented influences like *fear, rejection, worthlessness, shame, insecurity, defilement,* and *hopelessness.*

> *But thus you shall do to them: you shall **tear down their altars**, and **smash their sacred pillars**, and **hew down their Asherim**, and **burn their graven images with fire*** (Deuteronomy 7:5, emphasis added).

The instructions God gave to Moses told them to...

- "Tear down their altars." Locate and dismantle the pagan influences.
- "Smash their sacred pillars." Get rid of the things that remind them of those pagan influences.
- "Hew down their Asherim." Find and uncover places of darkness where these influences live.
- "Burn their graven images with fire." Purify and destroy the false images or lies about God and all that those images represent.

The instructions God gave to Moses for eliminating pagan influences in the Promised Land reflect, in principle, the process we use today to seek out and destroy the lies and controlling emotional influences that stem from past inner wounds—wounds that continue to limit us. We basically follow the same instructions: tear down, smash, hew down, and burn. Altars, pillars, Asherim, and fire represent parts of the process of emotional healing. They are as follows:

> *Altar*—An altar represents the influences that cause us to feel controlling negative emotions today, such as fear, rejection, etc.

Pillar—A pillar represents an emotional echo or triggering event that causes us to feel what we feel.

Asherim—Asherim represents the hidden dark place in the past where the lie was first planted.

Fire—Fire represents the truth of God that destroys the lies we have believed and that control us.

If we are to be free of controlling emotional influences, then we must find out *what* we feel, *when* we feel it, *why* we tend to feel or be controlled by that emotion, and what the healing *truth* is. It is a process that starts in the present, reflects the past, and leads us to the future.

The Lord instructed Moses to tear down the altars of the people whom the Israelites were to displace. That is what we need to do when a strong negative emotion binds us and causes us to live short of the abundance God intends for us. We need to tear down those altars.

"Tear Down Their Altars"

An altar was a place where blood or life was presented. It was a place of submission and control where the worshiper presented his or her life and hope to a deity. The gods that these seven nations worshiped were false gods. In other words, they did not exist. Each one simply represented a false idea about the true God. They were lies that engendered fear and performance rather than the love and acceptance that are available in God.

When we tear down altars today, we discover and dismantle the power of the lies that control us and our emotions. As we discussed in the previous chapter, our emotions flow from what we believe. We *feel* what we *believe*, and we *live* what we *feel*. For example, if I believe the world is a dangerous place, then I feel fear or insecurity. That fear then keeps me locked up and barricaded behind the walls of my house.

Again, if we are to dismantle the lies that control us, we must first find out what is controlling us. Is it fear, rejection, or shame? We can begin to get an idea of the lies that control us by looking at how we live and what we feel. These controlling lies are on display every day. Think of the person who never went to college because he was told he was not smart enough, or the one who abused her children because she was abused. Whatever the lie, it will direct us down prescribed paths that lead us away from God.

Sometimes only one emotion seems to control us, such as the *shame* that controlled my wife, Carol, and kept her limited around the belief that she just couldn't do anything well enough. Remember the man in the argument about the car? His life was controlled by the lie that told him he was not safe somehow, and therefore he felt threatened any time someone disagreed with him.

The second part of this book is filled with word pictures extracted from the Bible that describe how ordinary people lived under the influence of certain lies and emotions. We will also examine each of the controlling influences mentioned in Deuteronomy 7, along with the emotional profile they create. However, for now, here is a very brief summary of each of them.

Altars—The Lies That Control Us

Fear is based on the lie that we are all alone in dangerous waters. It is the first emotion mentioned in the Bible and the root of all other negative emotions. Fear makes us want to run and hide. When we are controlled by fear, we avoid life. We don't take chances or experience anything new. We tremble at the thought of what might be around the next corner.

Rejection is the lie that we don't fit in, that we don't belong. When we feel rejected, we seem to wander around in a state of anonymous confusion as to who and what we are. When rejection controls us, we sit by the wall waiting for someone to sign our dance card, all the time believing no one ever will.

Worthlessness is exactly that—the lie that we are worth less than others to whom we compare ourselves. We look at those around us and believe that we are not as good as they are. When we live under worthlessness, we spend most of our time striving to prove that we are worth the air and the space we consume. Seldom do we get to any place of self-worth.

Shame is the lie that we have crossed the line of God's grace, that we are not worthy of His love. Shame is like a toxic mud made up of failure that tells us we are not good enough. It makes us hang our heads and cover our faults like Adam and Eve, who tried to cover their nakedness with fig leaves. Shame also can apply outside the moral law of God and extend to any part of our lives where we believe we are "not good enough." Shame blocks us from intimacy with God and keeps us focused on our shortcomings.

Insecurity is the lie that says everything is a threat and no one is in control. Those under the lie of insecurity are constantly on the watch for the next wave of attacks. They live in a limping unsafety, believing they are helpless victims whose life and world are out of control. When we feel out of control, we try to find ways to take control of everything and everyone using every tool from emotional manipulation to addictions of all kinds. Shame keeps us in "Fortress Us." We trust nobody.

Defilement is the lie that tells us that it's over, that we are ruined for life. Defilement happens when an innocent victim is abused by someone he or she should have been able to trust. People who live under defilement believe they will never be the same again. They live with a dirty feeling. They wear the guilt of the one who sinned against them and find it difficult to experience intimacy of any kind.

Hopelessness is the lie that tells us we will never…whatever it is, we will never…. Those who are hopeless see the cup half empty without any way of refilling it. Hopelessness leaves us stooped over and stuck looking into blackness. When we live under the influence of hopelessness, we just quit.

All of us experience most of these emotions in the course of our lives, but when they begin to control us and interfere with all that God has for us, we need to deal with them. We need to *tear them down.*

Tearing something down means dismantling it. The altars that control us were built one wound at a time, just like an altar of stone is built one stone at a time. As a result, we have to tear them down one stone at a time. The Hebrew word translated as "tear down," *nathats*, implies that the influences that control us were built up and now must be torn down the same way, over a period of time.

We can know what influence is controlling us by what we feel. Emotions are the medium by which our minds interpret the world around us. What we feel about things, events, and people, is based on what we *believe* about them. It is not as simple as saying, "I'm afraid" or "I'm ashamed." There are a host of emotions and feelings that flow from the influence that controls us. These feelings are listed in the chapters that describe the various influences.

"Smash Their Sacred Pillars"

The pillars referred to in Deuteronomy 7:5 were a kind of memorial or image of the deity associated with the altar. It was a reminder of the lie that that deity represented. In our application, a pillar represents a trigger that reminds us of the lie we believe, which results in the emotions we feel. These triggers are like the "emotional echoes" referred to in the previous chapter. They are the *when* we feel *what* we feel.

For example, someone living under the lie of rejection may go to a family reunion and end up sitting all alone. He or she feels out of place at such a social function. Chances are, the other family members at the reunion have no idea that the person feels rejected by them. They may, in fact, say that this person does not like the family or is aloof. We need to be careful how we judge someone's heart. We are usually wrong. Perhaps when the rejected person was very young, he or she was left to be raised by a relative. Though that child may have been cared for, he or she still feels out of place. Now, anytime there is a family function, that person is reminded of the abandonment and feels rejected. The reunion is the *pillar*—the triggering event that reminds the person of the lie that he or she doesn't belong.

We run into these triggering pillars all day long. They may be as simple as a similar name or physical appearance of another person or place. They may be a familiar smell. For example, when I smell mothballs, I think of my maternal grandmother.

When my brother and I were very young, we used to go to her house, and many times we took a nap there. I'm not sure now as I write, whether that was because *we* needed a rest or my *grandmother* did. In any event, at naptime my grandmother would go to her cedar chest and pull out this gray woolen blanket with blue dots on it. We would curl up in the blanket and someone—either us or our grandmother—got to rest. The mothballs or the smell of that cedar chest is a *pillar* that releases warm and loving feelings in my memory.

There are many other pillars that evoke feelings of terror or shame. For example, a woman who has been sexually abused may feel trapped any time she is in a small room with any man. That small room triggers feelings of fear because it reminds her of a place where she was abused. Whatever the pillar, it is a reminder of a lie or a belief that controls our lives.

We are instructed to smash these sacred pillars. The Hebrew word translated as "smash" here is *shabar*, which means to crush or to break into pieces. When we smash these pillars, we break their ability to control and divert us. How do we smash these reminders of pain? We need to look to the times in our present-day lives when we tend to feel the strong emotions that take control of us. Maybe I feel fear when I enter a crowded room, or maybe I feel ashamed any time my spouse and I discuss intimacy. Remember, when we talk about tearing down altars, we find *what* we feel that stems from a lie we believe. When we smash pillars, we determine *when* we feel that way.

When do we feel rejected? *When* do we feel shameful? *When* do we feel hopeless and depressed? These times are the sacred pillars, which are more like those brightly colored plastic cones that restrict us in construction areas. When we know what we feel and when we feel it, we can begin to trace them to a source.

"Hew Down Their Asherim"

The King James Version translates *Asherim* as "groves," which is a good picture of what they really were. These were groves of trees—places where light was blotted out and truth obscured. They were places of secret sinning in Canaanite religion.

For our purpose, the Asherim is the place of darkness in the past *where* a wound occurred and a lie was enabled.

The limiting lies we believe in the present, as well as the emotions that accompany them, are rooted somewhere in the past. It is not always obvious why we believe or feel what we do. Sometimes lies are rooted in sudden traumatic events; sometimes they are part of the environment in which we were raised. Either way, the Asherim are the distant reflective surfaces off of which emotional echoes bounce.

When we "hew down Asherim," we go to the place of darkness by asking the Lord, in prayer, to bring us a memory picture of where the lie and the controlling emotions are rooted. We want to find the place *where* we began to feel what we feel and so uncover the lies we believe. The use of the word *hew* implies going to a place where something living was planted and is still shooting its obscuring foliage into our present, obstructing our vision of God and the abundant life He intends for us. When we find this place, we cut it down like a tree that hangs over our house, threatening to crash through the roof.

Sometimes more than one memory will surface where the lie is expressed. In that case we try to find the oldest memory in which the lie was rooted. However, sometimes a lie is so much a part of our culture or past that we cannot locate the very first time we began to believe that lie and take on the emotions associated with it. It is not as important to find the oldest memory as much as it is to find the place where the false beliefs and emotions are clearly represented. In that case, when the lie is uncovered, it is uncovered everywhere and anywhere it was alive. What we are looking for when we hew down Asherim is a place where we can uncover the source of the lie and bring truth to it, which brings us to the last part of the process God outlined for us to destroy the limiting lies that bind us.

"Burn Their Graven Images With Fire"

The ultimate method of purifying anything is through *fire*. Fire can remove anything that is not pure or true. When we want to remove impurities from gold, we subject it to fire to melt it down. The heat and the fire separate what is gold (what is eternal) from what is dross (imperfections, things that are not gold). In the same way, we submit the lies we believe to the fire of God's truth to separate them and allow truth to emerge. Anything that can be burned is not eternal, or of God.

There is fire all through the Old Testament, especially in the Torah. It was fire that purified Sodom and Gomorrah (see Gen. 19:24). God revealed Himself to Moses in a burning bush (see Ex. 3:2). It was fire that led the Israelites' way in the wilderness (see Ex. 14:24). It was fire that accompanied the presence of God on Mount Sinai (see Ex. 19:18). It was fire that consumed flesh, the carnality of the sacrifice (see Ex. 29:18).

Fire represents the holiness and purity of God, and especially the truth of His Word. We hear His Word from the midst of the fire (see Deut. 4:36). It is the truth of God's Word that incinerates and separates the lies from the truth.

After we discover *what* lies control us, *when* they control us, and *where* they were planted, we submit those lies to the *truth* of God. In fact, we submit them to the truth of God as expressed in His manifested presence in the memory picture. Quoting Scripture is great, but the presence of God in the truth is what incinerates the lies. The Bible says, "The Lord reigns; let the earth rejoice; let the many islands be glad. Clouds and thick darkness surround Him; righteousness and justice are the foundation of His throne. Fire goes before Him, and burns up His adversaries round about" (Ps. 97:1-3). Those "adversaries" or enemies are the things that keep us away from God. They are *fear, rejection, worthlessness, shame, insecurity, defilement,* and *hopelessness*— the "ites" that inhabit the promise of abundant life in the presence of God.

Once the Lord has taken us to a root memory where the lie is contained, we simply ask Him to reveal to us His presence and the truth regarding the situation in the memory picture. It is the fiery presence of the truth of God that incinerates and destroys the presence of the lie. No lie can withstand the presence of God.

But who can endure the day of His coming? And who can stand when He appears? For He is like a refiner's fire and like fullers' soap (Malachi 3:2).

The Sound of Truth

We might ask how we can know whether God is the one speaking to us, or if it is our own human thoughts, or even if it is the enemy. The best way to discern what we are hearing is to keep in mind this simple fact: The truth of God reflects the character of God. We can know something is the truth of God's Word to us by the character and effect of it. Psalm 19:7-10 gives us a good idea of the character of God's truth. In this psalm there are several synonyms for the communication of God: the law, testimony, precepts, commandment, fear, and the judgments of God. We can listen to what we hear and compare it to the sound of truth in this psalm.

*The law of the Lord is **perfect, restoring the soul;** the testimony of the Lord is **sure, making wise the simple.** The precepts of the Lord are **right, rejoicing the heart;** the commandment of the Lord is **pure, enlightening the eyes.** The fear of the Lord is **clean, enduring forever;** the judgments of the Lord are **true;** they are **righteous altogether.** They are **more desirable than gold,** yes, than much fine gold; sweeter also than honey and the drippings of the honeycomb* (Psalm 19:7-10, emphasis added).

Psalm 19 is a description of God's voice and what He is likely to say to us. It is a description of the Torah, and uses several different words such as *law*, or *testimony*; but for our purpose here, each one is just another way of saying, God's voice is:

- **Perfect, restoring the soul.**

This word for "perfect" is the Hebrew word *tamiym*, which describes a state of wholeness. When God speaks, it is meant to bring wholeness. God does not speak in a way that tears me down but in words that will ultimately lead to my healing and restoration. Yes, God speaks to us to discipline us when we need it. But even those words are tempered with mercy. In His wrath He always remembers mercy (see Hab. 3:2). God's words to us always draw us back to His bosom. Those words that push us away from His heart are not God's words. The words of God are the words of a *perfect* Father who has a *perfect* love for His children. He does not speak to us out of some kind of insecurity nor does He try to manipulate us with threats and fear.

God's voice leads us to restoration or perhaps conversion. He invites us into His heart and presence. It doesn't seem likely that God would invite us by greeting us with a stick. I would sum it up by saying that the words I hear from God are healing words that invite me to greater intimacy with Him.

- ### *Sure, making wise the simple.*

When God speaks, He does so with clarity. "God is not a God of confusion but of peace..." (1 Cor. 14:33). If we agree that God leads us through what He says, then what possible purpose would there be for Him to speak with confusion? God speaks in clear and uncluttered language, not shrouded in darkness and mystery.

God will not speak in a way that paralyses me and prevents me from moving toward Him or into His purposes. He speaks in a way that gives me confidence to respond to His voice. Imagine getting an invitation in the mail that doesn't tell you what you are invited to or where. Again, God's desire is that we draw near to Him. He does not play mind games with us. His Word has been compared to a light for us. "Your word is a lamp to my feet, and a light to my path " (Ps. 119:105). To be sure, God does not always give us the whole picture or all the details, but He will always lead us to the next step.

God invites us and leads us to Himself. When He speaks to us, His words and meaning are clear and give us confidence to respond to what He says.

- ### *Right, rejoicing the heart.*

God's voice has a kind of resonance about it. Anything that the Lord speaks to us has a right ring to it. The word "right" here is the Hebrew word *yashar*, which is a kind of ethical and moral rightness. The literal meaning is straight. When God speaks to us, He is leading us in simplicity to what would please Him. It's that kind of feeling we get when we study hard for a spelling test and know that we have the whole list down cold. There is a confidence in what we hear—that it is right.

The Lord's voice leads us in a way that agrees with His nature. He speaks to us in a way that reflects the needs and hearts of other people. God does not compromise Himself or His Word; indeed, He cannot contradict Himself. He is the Lord God, the Creator! He does not change His nature on a whim. He is not intimidated by our opinion of Him. He is completely holy and above our opinions.

There is a resonance in our hearts when God speaks—a feeling of joy that is not dependent on circumstances. When we hear God, the Lord brings us to a place where we are settled and at rest. Our heart rejoices with His heart because we agree with Him that we belong to Him.

- ***Pure, enlightening the eyes.***

When we say that God's voice is pure, we mean that it is obviously free of any impurity, but also, and perhaps more importantly, we are saying that God's voice is free of any mixed motive. God has chosen to love us, and when He tells us that He loves us, He is not leading us on. We need not wait for the other shoe to fall.

The effect of the purity of God's motives and love toward us *helps us to see ourselves as He sees us.* When the Bible uses the phrase "enlightening the eye," it is talking about our mind. When God tells us what He thinks and feels about us, our hearts and attitudes change. We live as the beloved of God, and so we are.

- ***Enduring…true…righteous…clean—giving me confidence and peace.***

When God speaks to us, He is not interested in the mundane. He does not go through our sock drawer or put on a white glove to see how often we dust. God is an eternal God and speaks to us about eternal things. What He says to us is solid, enduring, eternal, and righteous. There is an unchangeableness about the voice of God.

When God speaks to me, He draws me into the realm of eternity with Him. The psalmist said, "Forever, O Lord, Your word is settled in heaven. Your faithfulness continues throughout all generations; You established the earth, and it stands. They stand this day according to Your ordinances, for all things are Your servants" (Ps. 119:89-91). God speaks out of His faithfulness, and everything leads back to and holds together in Him. He is not going to change His mind. This gives me peace and confidence to believe all He says about Himself and me.

- ***Desirable…sweet—drawing me close to His heart.***

Finally, the voice of God carries with it sweetness. It is milk and honey to me. God has promised to bring us to the land of milk and honey. My good friend, Dr. Donald Wright has said that this is the place of intimate worship of God. "Your lips, my bride, drip honey; honey and milk are under your tongue…" (Song 4:11). Worship is our response to the heart of God.

This psalm also tells us that His Word is "desirable." Desirable means that there is a receptivity of the Word. The tenor of God's Word does not lead to a pit of despair where we wallow in our sin and separation from God. He always brings us back to Him. If what we hear does not lead us back to God, it is not God! God doesn't condemn us, though He will frequently confront us. When God does confront us, it is because He wants to remove anything that separates us from Him. We are drawn back again to His sweetness as we are drawn to honey.

Summary of the Character of God's Voice and the Effect of God's Voice

- Healing / Inviting me to God Himself.
- Clear / Allowing me to respond.
- Right / Giving me joy.
- Pure / Enlightening me about myself.
- Enduring / True, righteous, clean—giving me confidence.

- Desirable / Sweet—drawing me close, resulting in worship.

Another passage from the Word summarizes what we are saying:

> *But the wisdom* [whatever God speaks to us] *that comes from heaven is first of all* **pure**. *It is also* **peace loving**, **gentle** *at all times, and* **willing to yield to others**. *It is* **full of mercy** *and good deeds. It shows* **no partiality** *and is always* **sincere**. *And those who are peacemakers will plant seeds of* **peace** *and reap a harvest of* **goodness** (James 3:17-18 NLT, emphasis added).

When we have *listened*, as God has *spoken* in a way that agrees with the indications we have listed, then we are free to *respond*. And anything that God is leading us into will bring glory to Him and enrapture our hearts to fall more deeply in love with Him.

When we hear the truth of God, it will reflect the character of God and bring us to the awareness of the presence of God. In His presence there is healing from all the lies and wounds that bind us. We are free to live in His presence and to enjoy rest and peace, communion and shared purpose.

The Voice of Truth

God reveals His healing truth to us in an unlimited number of ways; we need to pay attention and listen carefully to hear Him. Whatever way God chooses to speak, it is always clear and unambiguous to the listener. God is not out to trick us. Why would God lead us to healing, then make His truth so complicated that we don't get it? God wants to speak to us, and He will do so in a way that is clear and life-bringing.

Also, do not limit what the Lord says or how He says it. We have heard the Lord speak in words of Scripture, through sensations such as warmth or light, and sometimes by just the feeling of a surrounding presence. Sometimes the Lord has brought other memories to us that contain the truth He is speaking to us. I have ministered to some who saw the faces of other people who represented what the Lord was saying. The key to hearing the truth that God is speaking in a memory picture is to listen and just receive it, not try to figure out what He will say. It is not a cognitive process as much as a spiritual experience. You might say that *if we want to hear God, we need to be out of our minds.* God may not say what we *think* He will say, but He will always say what we *need* Him to say.

Hearing the voice of God is not the province of a privileged and especially holy few. It is the right of all children of God in Christ who are led of the Spirit. God has longed to speak to us and heal us. We must listen with an open and rested heart, expecting God to bring the fire to burn up the lies that have kept us bound. *He will do it!*

When we have done all these things, the enemy and the lies he speaks have no place to run and no place to hide. We do not have to spend a lot of time shouting at demons. Demons cannot survive in the presence of Truth, which is in fact the presence of God. When the Truth shows up, the enemy must flee.

When I was in my late 20's, I lived in a nice apartment outside Latrobe, Pennsylvania. The only downfall about the apartment was the field across from it in which people had dumped old furniture and junk. All that trash brought the presence of rats, which occasionally scurried across the parking lot. It was unsettling, to say the least.

One day the landlord brought in a backhoe and hauled out several truckloads of trash. When the trash was removed, so were the rats. Demons are the rats, and the lies are the trash that litters our lives. If you will get rid of the trash, or the lies, then the rats, the demons, will go away.[1]

When we have heard the truth and have taken out the trash, we need to consider the current triggering event and apply the same truth to it. Whatever was true in the past is now true there as well. The peace we found in the past now fills the present and becomes a promise from God into the future.

---

1.   I was reminded of my own personal experiences with rats as I read *Deep Wounds, Deep Healing* by Charles Kraft, page 258.

What follows is a very abbreviated version of a typical ministry session, so that you can see it broken into its various components. This sample is not all you need to know to facilitate ministry to other people, but rather a picture of the flow of the ministry as we have experienced it. Once again, I suggest that you seek training from others who are competent and experienced in inner healing before you attempt to facilitate this ministry.

Sample Ministry Session

Lester was a man in his late 50's who was referred to us by a friend. He was an affable man with a southern charm and wit. I had seen him many times over the years, and his most pronounced feature was his warm smile. However, Lester was not smiling this day. All his smiles had given way to a sober seriousness.

We opened the time together by welcoming the presence of the risen and exalted Christ, remembering His promise that "where two or three have gathered together in My name, I am there in their midst" (Mt. 18:20).

Altar

Lester was feeling hopeless and rejected. As we walked through the emotional profile, feelings of rejection were verified.

Pillar

We discussed what Lester was feeling, and I asked about a recent time when he experienced those feelings. He related the scene of his wife's leaving him without explanation. He recounted how she said she was going to work, but then called him to say she was not coming home. Lester was shocked and felt utterly rejected. He rehearsed over and over again the many times he had been rejected.

As Lester recalled the present experience, I asked him, "What do you feel as you look at this recent memory picture?"

Lester replied, "I feel alone—I will always be alone."

Asherim

With his feelings clarified, we prayed, "Lord, take Lester by the hand and lead him to the source of these feelings and beliefs he is experiencing today." With that, the Lord brought Lester to a memory of growing up in a very large family where he was one of ten children. He was kind of lost in the shuffle. The memory picture was one of Lester being taken out of his family and asked to live with an older couple who needed help. Lester moved in with them and was separated from his family. He would come home regularly, but he felt increasingly out of place—disconnected— like he no longer belonged.

When Lester finished describing the memory picture, I once again asked him, "Lester, what do you feel as you look at this picture?" Lester quickly replied as he did in the recent event with his wife, "I feel alone—I'll always be alone—I don't belong anywhere."

Fire

With that we asked the Lord to reveal His presence and truth to Lester. In a few seconds Lester was aware of the presence of God in the form of words that were repeated over and over: "You belong to Me—You belong to Me. I have always been with you, and I will always be with you." Then Lester could sense the presence of the Lord in what could only be described as a warmth that felt like, "It's okay. It will be okay."

For a long time Lester had believed that somehow he was alone and that perhaps there was something unacceptable about him because his parents had sent him away and his wife had left him. When he began to experience the warmth of the presence of God that day, and the truth was revealed that God had a purpose for Lester living with that older couple, then an additional torrent of truth flooded his mind out of his memories. The Lord reminded Lester that because he did not live with his family, he did not become addicted to alcohol as his siblings had. In fact, the older couple whom he went to live with encouraged him to pursue things that his parents told him he could never do. God had a purpose in Lester. Lester was accepted and blessed in the presence of Christ who had always been with him.

After the flood of truth subsided, we asked Lester to think about that scene where his wife called him telling him that she was not coming home. Lester was able to forgive his wife and release her to the grace of God. As Lester recalled that recent time, he still felt sad at her leaving, but he was aware of the presence of God saying, "It's okay, Lester. I'm here."

Note to the Reader

As you move through the chapters in Part Two, you will have an opportunity to understand the nature and the emotional profiles of the lies that people live under. Then you will have an opportunity to go through the same process that Lester did in the presence of Christ, comparing your life to those of others in the Bible who felt just like you do. They were regular people who were hurt, had fears, felt rejected, and all the rest. You will be asked to compare your life to theirs and journal similar experiences and feelings. Then the Lord Jesus Himself will take you by the hand and bring you to the source of those memories for healing. The Lord will speak the truth to you, and you will be healed!

I pray right now for an awareness in your heart of God's intention to heal you. He longs to tell you that you are loved and accepted. Allow Him to take you by the hand and lead you to healing in His presence.

CHAPTER SIX

CHANGING THE LOCKS

Now when the unclean spirit goes out of a man, it passes through waterless places, seeking rest, and does not find it. Then it says, "I will return to my house from which I came"; and when it comes, it finds it unoccupied, swept, and put in order. Then it goes and takes along with it seven other spirits more wicked than itself, and they go in and live there; and the last state of that man becomes worse than the first. That is the way it will also be with this evil generation (Matthew 12:43-45).

A friend of mine told me a story about a man who owned a piece of property that he rented to some irresponsible tenants. They abused his trust and his property. They neglected to pay the rent, punched holes in the walls, and stained the carpets. Eventually, the owner of the house had no recourse but to ask the tenants to move. After a long legal hassle, the owner evicted them, cleaned the property, made the necessary repairs, added fresh paint, and installed new carpet so that it could be rented again to more responsible tenants.

A little while after he had finished the restoration, the owner was shocked to learn that in the middle of the night the former abusive tenants had moved back into his repaired and restored property. The owner had made a critical error—though his house had been cleaned and restored to rentable condition, he had forgotten to change the locks. Subsequently, the abusive tenants were able to move back into the house because they still had the keys!

When we experience God's presence in our wounded memories, we sweep the lies from our house and replace them with God's order that brings peace. But those lies will attempt to reenter our property. They will use their keys in the unchanged locks and move in to gain control of us again. So, in order to maintain healing, ownership, and order, and to remove the keys from the enemy's hands once and for all, we must invite a new Occupant— Jesus Christ.

In the passage of Scripture at the beginning of this chapter, Jesus told the religious types of His day that they had a well-ordered religious house, but one which had no tenant. They had refused His ownership. "He came to His own, and those who were His own did not receive Him" (Jn. 1:11).

Beloved, it is not enough just to hear the biblical truth that sweeps our hearts and minds free of the lies we have believed and sets things in proper order; we also need to invite a living tenant to move into our house. That tenant must be Christ Jesus.

One of the greatest concerns involved with healing is that lies are completely removed in order to maintain healing. It is possible to hear the truth and find healing, only to have the lies creep back into our lives along familiar ruts of thought and emotional response.

Those old tenants had left our hearts on a hostile basis, believing it was *their* house. In order to insure the lies that formerly controlled us aren't able to return and move in again, we must take the keys out of their hands. Three specific keys allow former lies to gain entrance and control: *unforgiveness, self-promises,* and *demonic strongholds.*

Because we have become accustomed to living with lies, self-promises, and the bitterness of unforgiveness, we have to be intentional about throwing them out. In doing so, we change the locks so they cannot reenter and control our lives. The enemy will not stop trying to regain entrance until we forcefully take the keys out of his hands, by releasing others from our judgment, by forgiveness, and by releasing ourselves from promises we made to ourselves when we were wounded.

Uncovering Self-Promises

When God instructed Moses to eliminate the evil influences from the Promised Land, He also warned him not to make any kind of covenant relationship with these influences that were displaced. The Lord said, "When the Lord your God delivers them before you and you defeat them, then you shall utterly destroy them. *You shall make no covenant with them* and show no favor to them" (Deut. 7:2, emphasis added). A covenant is a promise that binds us to another person, or in this case, a belief. When we are wounded, a controlling lie is implanted in our hearts. In the process of healing, we hear the truth that dispels the lies we have come to believe. Many times these lies are held in place by promises we make to ourselves.

Remember the little boy in the singing class in Chapter One. Because of his teacher's words, the little boy was shamed and embarrassed in front of his peers. A shame-based lie was planted, telling him that he fell short of expectations. He was "not good enough" to sing in the program or any other public communication.

Flowing from the lies implanted in our hearts are promises we make to ourselves. A self-promise is an agreement with ourselves that binds us—a promise we make to ourselves to live a certain way. For the most part, they are "I will" kinds of statements.

When we live under a particular *influence*, we make promises to ourselves to keep those beliefs in place, which cause us to repeat a pattern over and over again. For example, the little boy who lived under the influence of shame could have made a promise to himself never to be caught in a position of embarrassment again. Perhaps he promised himself never to trust anyone in authority and to always hide in the background, no matter what.

Self-promises are unique to each person and experience. Here are a few we have heard in ministry sessions.

- ❍ "I will not allow myself to get close to anyone."
- ❍ "I will not trust anyone in authority."
- ❍ "I will be loved by everyone."
- ❍ "I will not risk rejection."
- ❍ "I will always fail."
- ❍ "I will always be in control."
- ❍ "I won't let anyone see me."

○   "I will be perfect."
○   "I will take responsibility."
○   "I will earn love."

Each of the influences that control us inspire an infinite variety of self-promises as varied and unique as our fingerprints. The question we must ask the wounded child in us is "What did I promise myself as a result of the wound I received?"

The promises we make to ourselves usually show up in the way we live, and they become an operating system that governs our lives. For instance, I once sat with a woman who recalled an event that happened when she was in elementary school. Her parents who were very busy with their own lives and careers sent her to school a year too early; consequently, she struggled socially and educationally. Unable to please her teachers or her parents, the little girl promised herself, "I will not risk rejection by getting close to other people." The promise she made to herself reflected the lie she had come to believe that she was somehow unacceptable and destined to live on the outside. She never came close to the warmth of the fire and other people. Her self-promise actually held her on the outside, enabling her to live as a rejected one.

Self-promises influence not only the one who makes them but also future generations. The lies we tell ourselves are like seeds in an apple that bring forth more trees with more apples that contain more seeds of the same lies. It is a cycle of pain that will find its way into future generations.

The lies and resulting self-promises condition the hearts of our children. What we may refer to as "generational sin" is the collection of lies and self-promises and perhaps the bitterness or curses that come as a result. We hand down our emotional influence like granny's silverware. The Lord has warned us, "You shall make no covenant with them [the "ites" that live in the land representing fear, rejection, etc.]…you shall not intermarry with them…they will turn your sons away from following Me to serve other gods…" (Deut. 7:2b-4).

Consider a child growing up in a home with alcoholic parents where the atmosphere is chaotic and out of control. The insecurity of that home plants seeds of insecurity in the child's heart who grows up trying to control and manage his own life and the lives of his family resulting in more children who will carry the same seed of insecurity. We can produce no other fruit than what comes from the seed implanted in our own hearts. The influence of insecurity in that chaotic home led the children away from the face of God and into a life where they will feel the need to control every aspect of their lives, including their relationship with God.

Because of the Father's relentless passion for our faces, He will reveal and give us the grace to break these self-promises in the safety of His presence. We break them by recognizing and renouncing their power over our lives while confessing the truth.

Self-promises bind lies to our hearts. As we break these promises, we disrupt ungodly patterns that keep pain in our lives. Another factor that prevents our total healing and freedom is the bitterness that comes along with the pain of wounding. If we are to be free of the lies we have exposed, we must remove the bitterness and replace it with compassion.

Healing Forgiveness

When we have been offended or wounded, our hearts and attention are hijacked and focused on the wound. And as long as we are focused on the wound, we cannot be focused on God. Jesus said, "Blessed are the pure in heart, for they shall see God" (Mt. 5:8). Bitterness clogs the heart and flows from the wound like an infection, binding us to the one who has wounded us. The Lord deserves and commands that we love Him with all our hearts. Whatever portion of our hearts is filled with bitterness and judgment from wounding is a portion that we have taken from God. He wants it back!

Forgiveness is a legal transaction that releases those who wound us from our wrath. In addition, forgiveness removes bitterness and judgment we hold against the one who wounded us. Whereas, anger and judgment from past wounds keep the lies alive in our hearts. For example, consider the young boy who was told by his teacher that he could not sing and was embarrassed in front of his class. He probably didn't spend his life actively thinking about that day in singing rehearsal, but the wound resulted in a judgment in his heart against the teacher.

If you or I had a debt and failed to pay it for any reason, our creditor would probably resort to filing a document against us in the courthouse—a judgment. This judgment is held against us and limits our future credit until the debt is satisfied. Likewise, the wounded child in us holds a judgment in his heart against those who wounded him. The judgment not only limits the one who wounded us but limits us as well, as we hold the judgment against them. We are bound and limited by the same measure. Jesus said, "Do not judge so that you will not be judged. For in the way you judge, you will be judged; and by your standard of measure, it will be measured to you" (Mt. 7:1-2). Our judgments are weights placed on the opposite end of the scales of human justice to balance out our wounding. They are heavy and hold us back from moving on emotionally. We feel the weight of the judgments we hold as they separate us from the face of God as well as restored relationship with people.

The judgments against us are removed in Christ, and we are free to do the same with those who have offended us. We have heard much teaching on the power of forgiveness as it relates to healing broken lives and setting them free. Forgiveness is more than a legal transaction of release, however. It is the extension of God's own heart of compassion that removes demonic rights to our hearts.

Ultimately, forgiveness needs to replace the bitterness or fear in our hearts with compassion. Until we can see the one who wounded us with compassion, the way God sees them, we are not really free from the wound or the judgment that comes with it. They are off our hook but not off God's.[1]

We are able to forgive only when we have experienced the presence of God. Many times we have gotten to a place in the healing sessions where forgiveness is required to move forward, but the wounded one cannot release the one who hurt them. They are afraid to let them off the hook for fear they will be wounded again. We have learned that it is a lot easier for the wounded

---

1.   Neil T. Anderson, *Victory Over the Darkness, Second Edition* (Ventura, CA: Regal, 2000), p. 162.

children in us to extend grace and forgiveness when they are snuggled warmly in the lap of the Father where nothing can harm them. When we are safe in the lap of God, we are able to make others safe as well and release them from our judgment. Forgiveness not only removes judgment from our hearts, but it also removes the keys from the enemy's hands so that he cannot reoccupy our hearts.

We move now to the last key to maintaining freedom and that is evicting the demonic influence that has come into our lives as a result of past hurts. (I recommend reading *The Importance of Forgiveness* by John Arnott, published by Sovereign World, 1997.)

Pulling the Rug Out From Under the Devil

Lies, self-promises, and unforgiveness give the devil legal ground to live in our hearts and redirect our attention away from God. But when you expose satan's lie with God's truth, his power is broken. That is why Jesus said, "You shall know the truth and the truth shall make you free" (Jn. 8:32). Satan's lie cannot withstand the truth any more than the darkness of night can withstand the light of the rising sun. Deceiving spirits are like cockroaches. They come out only at night; when you turn off the light, they head for the shadows.

The role of the demonic is to ensure that the lies remain in a prominent place of our lives. Angels, including lucifer, were created to cover the presence of God who is pure Truth. "You were the *anointed cherub who covers*, and I placed you there. You were on the holy mountain of God; you walked in the midst of the stones of fire" (Ezek. 28:14). When lucifer and the other angels fell, they were still "covering"; but now, instead of the presence of Truth, they cover the presence of lies.

The Bible says of the devil and his demons, "He...does not stand in the truth because there is no truth in him. Whenever he speaks a lie, he speaks from his own nature, for he is a liar and the father of lies" (Jn. 8:44b). When we expose the lies we have believed, we remove the legal standing of the devil. The presence of God, the Truth, pulls the rug out from under the devil.

Demons have a legal right to protect lies until we expose the lies and bring them into the presence of God. When we expose the lies, we expose the enemy and remove their legal right to stand. The deliverance we experience is in fact delivering the Truth of the presence of Jesus Christ and evicting the demonic who live on lies.

Jesus was and is Truth in Person. When He walked down the street or into a synagogue, unclean spirits were confronted by pure Truth and said something like, "What business do we have with each other, Jesus of Nazareth? Have You come to destroy us? I know who You are—the Holy One of God!" (Mk. 1:24) There was no option; they had to leave town. They had encountered the Truth and had nowhere to stand. It is the presence of Truth that ultimately delivers us from the devil.

You will have an opportunity to change the locks at the conclusion of this book in the Personal Ministry Guide. When you change the locks, you will invite the Occupant to occupy His property. You have been bought with a price and belong to Him (see 1 Cor. 6:20).

There is an end to the story at the beginning of this chapter. When the owner discovered the abusive tenants had returned, he took radical action. Now a little wiser, he decided on a different course of action to remove the reckless intruders. He did not call the police or take the same legal action which he had previously done. Instead, the owner loaded a truck with his own furniture. After driving up to the front of his house, he began to unload his furniture and move it into his property. The people soon realized that the owner was serious about his property and willing to occupy the house so that they would leave. They packed up their belongings and left.

The lies, promises, and demonic influence who have cozened up in your heart are on borrowed time. Jesus is standing at the door of your heart and knocking even now.

CHAPTER SEVEN

LOOKING BOTH WAYS

O Lord, You have searched me and known me. You know when I sit down and when I rise up; You understand my thought from afar. You scrutinize my path and my lying down, and are intimately acquainted with all my ways. Even before there is a word on my tongue, behold, O Lord, You know it all. You have enclosed me behind and before, and laid Your hand upon me. Such knowledge is too wonderful for me; it is too high, I cannot attain to it (Psalm 139:1-6).

My family and I live in a quiet little town; even so, the traffic has always been very busy on Main Street. When our children were very small, I would never have dreamed of allowing them to cross that street by themselves. When we would come to the corner, we'd wait for the light to change from red to green so that we could safely cross. Once the light changed, however, we didn't just immediately set out across the street; we would look first to the right and then to the left to make sure that it was safe. What made it even more safe for my children was that they did not have to cross the street alone. Their little hands were in the hand of their father. Daddy was bigger and could see farther in both directions. It was safe to cross the street with their hands in Daddy's hand.

When we begin the inner-healing process, we cross over from lies to truth, from wounds to healing. Just as we hold hands when we cross the street, in the same manner we have a Father who takes our little, powerless hand, looking both ways before we cross. The Father looks to the left, our past, and then to the right, our future, and in the safety of His grip, the present, we cross over to healing. Because our heavenly Father is bigger than we are, He can see infinitely in both directions and knows exactly where He's taking us. Nothing takes Him by surprise. We can trust His grip on our hand—we can feel it as we cross over. Father will not leave us alone as we find healing.

Psalm 139 is a message to those who have placed their hands in the big hands of the Father to lead them over to healing and wholeness.

God's Knowing Hands

The original Hebrew word translated as "know" in Psalm 139:1-2 suggests the image of a hand that has covered and discovered us. The Hebrew word *yad* is also contained in the words for *power*, *authority*, *knowledge*, *provision*, or a hand that *forms* or *shapes* us like clay. God's hand—His power, His knowledge of us, His provision for us—encompasses our lives. Everything we are and everything we have experienced is in the hand of God, including past wounds. In the ecstasy of this reality, the psalmist begins with a word of praise: "O Lord." *Lord* is the personal name of God, *Yahweh*. This is the name by which Abraham referred to God. It is the name for the One who speaks with us in a personal, face-to-face way. The psalmist is saying something like this: "O Lord, I praise You because You have my life in Your hands...."

The psalm tells us that God knows us intimately. Even as I write these words and you read them, God is aware of your most intimate thoughts and concerns. He knows the reasons you had for picking up this book in the first place. His hand reaches into your inner recesses to the extent that there is nothing that He is not aware of. His hand has covered every inch of you, inside and out, whether you are aware of it or not. God's knowing hand is like an x-ray that you cannot see, but that looks into your deepest parts to find injury and brokenness. Such is the intimate searching of God.

If we are honest, most times we are not aware of God's knowing and loving hand around us. However, God's presence surrounds and fills everything at every time whether we are aware of Him or not. When Jacob, the son of Isaac, fled from

Esau, he traveled through the wilderness alone—or so he thought. Then he was awakened in the middle of the night with a vision of a ladder that went from Heaven to earth with angels ascending and descending. He was living in the presence of God and didn't know it, as the Bible says: "Surely the Lord is in this place, and I did not know it" (Gen. 28:16b). Although Jacob was not aware of God's presence, that didn't change the reality that He was there.

We also live in the interactive presence of God, whether we realize it or not. The room you are in right now as you read these words is filled with radio waves and TV broadcasts; you just can't see them or hear them because you don't have a suitable receiver. But they are there, nonetheless. So is God.

Not only does God know you intimately, but He also knows every aspect of your life. He knows when you sit down, when you get up, and all the rest. God is not removed from any part of your life or what concerns you, nor even from what you think. As we said in an earlier chapter, what we feel is a product of what we believe, and what we believe or think is a product of our experience. Some of those experiences have been good, and some of them have not been so good. Some of them were places of wounding, misunderstanding, or abuse. Even so, they are not news to God. He sees them even now and longs to pour out His healing oil upon them.

Between God's Hands

The most comforting image revealed in Psalm 139 is God enclosing us behind and before with His hand upon us. In other words, God looks both ways in our lives. The image is of our lives placed between the hands of God, which are cupped over us, guarding us gently as we would shield a flickering candle flame from the wind. God's left hand is facing His right hand, and we are in the middle. We are totally enclosed and protected between His hands. God holds the past, future, and present firmly and tenderly in the grip of His hand as we cross the street.

For those of us stuck in this veil of tears—in the human dimension—we must bend our minds around the concept that

God is not a dimensional being. God is not bound by time or space in any way. He exists outside them—He invented them—He is *Lord* of them. God is present everywhere and all the time at every instant. The Bible gives us a fuller idea of God's omnipresent perspective.

For a thousand years in Your sight are like yesterday when it passes by, or as a watch in the night (Psalm 90:4).

But do not let this one fact escape your notice, beloved, that with the Lord one day is like a thousand years, and a thousand years like one day (2 Peter 3:8).

...I am God, and there is no other; I am God, and there is no one like Me, declaring the end from the beginning, and from ancient times things which have not been done... (Isaiah 46:9-10).

It is important to know that God is, in effect, still alive in the past to bring us healing in the present. Because time or space does not limit God, He exists in the past, future, and present all at the same time. The reality is that *God is still alive in the past to bring us healing.* He can look to the left and see when we were abused or when we began to believe false things about ourselves or God, and then He delivers truth and healing. God was there, and He is still there in that place when someone wounded us, whether or not we were aware of Him. And what is more, God can see the future from the past. Whatever God speaks to us as truth in that past wounding is still true as a *promise in the future.* If I was not alone in the past, I will never be alone in the future.

The God Who Is Here and There

The psalmist asks a question: "Where can I go from Your Spirit? Or where can I flee from Your presence?" (Ps. 139:7)

The simple answer is, there is nowhere we can go away from God's presence—not even the past.

If I ascend to heaven, You are there; if I make my bed in Sheol, behold, You are there. If I take the wings of the *dawn, if I dwell in the remotest part of the sea, **even there Your hand will lead me**, and Your right hand will lay hold of me. If I say, "Surely the darkness will over-whelm me, and the light around me will be night," even the darkness is not dark to You, and the night is as bright as the day. Darkness and light are alike to You* (Psalm 139:8-12, emphasis added).

Even when we are in total darkness of remembered abuse—a time when we could not sense the presence of God—God was and is with us. God will not let go of our hands even in remembered times of abuse. To be sure, it's hard to reconcile how the presence of God would be in that place of great abuse. But He was there.

The most common and logical question asked by abused people is, "If God was really there, why did He allow me to be abused? Why didn't He stop it?" To answer this question we have to consider again that God does not exist in nor is He limited to time and space as we understand them. God did not want that abuse to happen, nor did He specifically allow you to be abused or wounded. Someone else chose to hurt you, and God does not override free will. If someone wants to sin, God will allow it, but He does not want it. God could have stopped Eve from taking that first bite, but He did not. She took it, and as a result she was separated from the presence of God.

What is true is that even in those days of great abuse and wounding, God saw a day of healing. He saw you reading these words right now. God is both here in the present with you and there in the past simultaneously. The presence of the Lord fills the past memories of abuse. As you remember those times, He is there ahead of you—waiting to bring truth and healing to your heart.

It is important to understand that God's right hand, His hand of power, is leading you to healing. As you begin the process of inner healing, allowing God's hand to search you, He will remind you of times of wounding. These memories, these pictures, will not be pleasant to look at. Some will cause fear and put you back in touch with the source of pain in your life. Thankfully, God is the one who brings these painful memory pictures to you in order to bring truth and to heal the wounds they contain. God is not stirring up pain to punish you, but to extinguish it.

You cannot change history. The things that have happened to you are real and painful. When you are hurt physically, the open wound is painful. But as healing comes, the wound closes while a scar remains. Although the scar is a reminder of the pain, there is no actual pain because the wound is healed.

At this point the healed wounds of the past become tools in the hands of God for healing in other lives. They make us sensitive to others who have been wounded like us. As a result, we are able to "comfort those who are in any affliction with the comfort with which we ourselves are comforted by God" (2 Cor. 1:4b). God does not waste anything. The wounds that we may think disqualify us, in fact, become our qualification—our redemptive résumé. Who could better understand someone who has been wounded than one who has been wounded the same way? Many individuals who come through our ministry later become involved in bringing healing to others. It is a God thing and proof of healing.

At the end of Psalm 139, the psalmist invites God to search him again:

> *Search me, O God, and know my heart; try me and know my anxious thoughts; and see if there be any hurtful way in me, and lead me in the everlasting way* (Psalm 139:23-24).

For the remainder of this book, we will invite God to search us, to discover those areas of wounded weakness, to decipher the thoughts that are not God's thoughts, and root out any influence that robs us of intimacy with God. We will examine the various influences we live under, the altars to which our lives have been presented. We'll look at "pictures" of people in the Bible who struggled with the same things we do and who were wounded the same ways we have been. Into those pictures we'll see the presence of God flow in the fullness of grace and truth. And whatever was true for those saints will become true for us as well.

At the end of each chapter you will be directed to the Personal Ministry Guide at the end of the book to compare your life and emotions with those of people in the Bible. Then you can ask God to bring to mind those places where anxious thoughts and wounds were implanted in your life. Allow the Lord to bring them to you. Don't work at remembering; just relax and receive the memory picture from God. Where God takes you, God intends to heal you. He will not let go of your hand.

Before you begin this process—before you read each of the following chapters—bathe yourself in the presence of God in prayer. Then, read the chapters, acknowledging God's love and desire for your healing and intimacy with Him. It is the presence of God that brings truth, order, and peace to your wounded emotions. Again, we suggest that those who have serious controlling emotional issues seek out additional help from those trained in the ministry of inner healing. Read each of the following chapters with an open spirit acknowledging the presence of God.

Those who have read this material or who have participated in ministry sessions have commented that it was the emphasis on and the careful walking in the presence of God that made the difference for them. They experienced powerful healing and deliverance, and they also experienced the gentleness of His compassion and love.

Note that the Hebrew words for *compassion* and *womb* are related words.[1] When God described Himself in Exodus 34:6, He listed compassion first: "Then the Lord passed by in front of him and proclaimed, 'The Lord, the Lord God, compassionate and gracious, slow to anger, and abounding in lovingkindness and truth.' "

We are, in effect, in the womb of His love as He pours out His compassion upon us, bringing us to Himself and healing, just

---

1.   Strong's O.T. reference number 7358 and 7356. See also the Greek word for compassion, Strong's N.T.: 4697, *splagchnizomai* (splangkh-nid´-zom-ahee); middle voice from N.T.: 4698; to have the bowels yearn, i.e. (figuratively) feel sympathy, to pity.

as it was the overflowing compassion in the heart of Jesus that preceded His healing virtue (see Mt. 20:34; Mk. 1:41). Take time to invite the presence of God as you prayerfully read the following chapters. Allow the Lord Himself to carry you through to deliverance as a mother would carry the child who is formed in her womb.

Look Both Ways

As you work through the next chapters, remember that God looks both ways. He knows what has happened in your past, what is happening now, and what will happen in your future. Whatever the Lord speaks to you in the past is true today and will be His promise to you in the future. Take it and the additional Scriptures each chapter presents as God's promises. Let them become praise in your mouth as you find healing in the presence of God.

> *Remember this, and be assured; recall it to mind, you transgressors. Remember the former things long past, for I am God, and there is no other; I am God, and there is no one like Me, declaring the end from the beginning, and from ancient times things which have not been done, saying, "My purpose will be established, and I will accomplish all My good pleasure"* (Isaiah 46:8-10).

Let's agree with David and say, "O God, You have searched me, and You know me. Continue to search me and know me. I will know You better as Your hand holds my hand, directing and healing me. In all times and in all places, Lord, You won't let me go."

PART TWO

THE PROCESS OF HEALING WOUNDED HEARTS

CHAPTER EIGHT

ARE YOU AFRAID OF THE DARK?

Fear

Now Ahab told Jezebel all that Elijah had done, and how he had killed all the prophets with the sword. Then Jezebel sent a messenger to Elijah, saying, "So may the gods do to me and even more, if I do not make your life as the life of one of them by tomorrow about this time." And he was afraid and arose and ran for his life and came to Beersheba, which belongs to Judah, and left his servant there. But he himself went a day's journey into the wilderness, and came and sat down under a juniper tree; and he requested for himself that he might die, and said, "It is enough; now, O Lord, take my life, for I am not better than my fathers." He lay down and slept under a juniper tree; and behold, there was an angel touching him, and he said to him, "Arise, eat." Then he looked and behold, there was at his head a bread cake baked on hot stones, and a jar of water. So he ate and drank and lay down again. The angel of the Lord came again a second time and touched him and said, "Arise, eat, because the journey is too great for you." So he arose and ate and drank, and went in the strength of that food forty days and forty nights to Horeb, the mountain of God. Then he came there to a cave and lodged there; and behold, the word of the Lord came to him, and He said to him, "What are you doing here, Elijah?" He said, "I have been very zealous for the Lord, the God of hosts; for the sons of Israel have forsaken Your covenant, torn down Your altars and killed Your prophets with the sword. And I alone am left; and they seek my life, to take it away" (1 Kings 19:1-10).

The Portrait of Fear

It was cold and dark. The searing heat of the desert through which he had run all day had given way to an unforgiving rawness that penetrated to the very core of the man lying in the black of night. He had run as far as his legs and the light could carry him. Just as his strength was running out, he spotted a small tree—a bush, really. Taking his last labored steps, he carried himself to the tree and collapsed at its roots. In his exhaustion he gasped out a labored and breathless request, "Lord, let me die."

As he lay there, his mind was filled with the scenes of the previous days. He was the one who had stood upon Mount Carmel defying hundreds of priests of Baal—taunting them in their futile cries to a nonexistent god. He was the one who had called down the fire of God's presence to consume the well-watered carcass of his offering. And the blood was scarcely dry on his sword, with which he had slain those hundreds of false priests fattened at Jezebel's table. It was him! *Him*!

Then, with one little word, a harlot queen had breathed a threat to him as false as the gods she served. And all he could see was fear—*terror*. He ran and ran—and ran right out of his country and into the wilderness of Judah beyond her grasp and into the lap of Yahweh. Now his tortured mind and body were trembling at the prospect of royal revenge as he muttered, "Please, Lord, let me die."

Suddenly his shallow sleep was disrupted by the jostling of someone saying, "Wake up, wake up." As he came to his senses, he could smell bread baking on hot stones. Opening his eyes, he spied a jar of water that had been placed next to him. There beside him was all that he would need to survive in this place of self-imposed exile.

The one who had awakened him stayed with him. "Eat up; you need your strength for the journey," he advised. As Elijah felt strength returning to his body, he set out on a journey of several days to Mount Horeb, the mountain of God, the place of God's heart. Elijah climbed the desert slope and came to a cave where he sat down again in the darkness. As he grew still, the word of the Lord came to him, saying, "What's the matter, Elijah?"

Elijah replied, "Lord, I've done the best I can do, and it's not enough. Now they want to kill me. Nobody understands. *I am alone.*"

The Influence of Fear

Fear seems to throw itself in front of us at every turn, making us want to run away and hide under the bed in solitude. The lie that inspires fear is that we *are alone*. Living under the influence of fear will cause you to spend your life running away and avoiding, as Adam did at the fall. What a difference it would make to be able to see the presence of God amidst our fearful circumstances.

Fear is an emotion that has the capability of shattering us, freezing us in our tracks, or melting us into ineffective paralysis. Fear is stationed like a sentinel at the frontier of all new things that we could do or experience in God. It was fear that caused an entire nation to shrink back from the abundant life in God's land of promise in Numbers chapters 13–14. Fear always seems to pop up when something new or unfamiliar is about to happen. We refer to it as "fear of the unknown," but in reality it is more a fear that God will not be there with us in that new place.

The first nation mentioned in Deuteronomy chapter 7 that the Lord would deliver before Israel was the Hittites. The word *Hittite* springs from the Hebrew word *chatath*, which is one of the words for fear. This is fear in the sense of being broken or shattered by impending terror; it literally means "to tremble." The Hittites were a fearsome and warlike people known for their brutality to those whom they conquered. *Chatath* is frequently translated as "dismayed" or "discouraged" and is used in synonymous parallelism with the word fear.

Fear is the oldest and first emotion mentioned in the Bible. Adam told God, "I heard the sound of You in the garden, and I was afraid because I was naked..." (Gen. 3:10). Adam was afraid because, for the first time since his creation, he faced the world alone and in his own power. He also was afraid of the consequences of his sin. His fear was the result of his separation from God. Fear is the strongest of all the emotions we experience.

I believe that God listed fear as the first influence we encounter because it is the strongest negative influence and keeps us separated from God and His purpose for us.

Fear entered the world after man sinned against God, shattering the peaceful communion he enjoyed with God. Man saw that he was "naked"—on his own and apart from God—and hid at the prospect of this separation. It is the very root and origin of all the other emotions we will talk about in this book: rejection, worthlessness, shame, insecurity, defilement, and hopelessness.

Emotional Profile of Fear

Fear creates its own unique emotional profile in us. When we live under the trembling influence of fear we feel...

Afraid

It seems obvious or redundant to say that if we live under fear, we feel afraid. But it's not as obvious as you think. To be afraid is to be filled with and controlled utterly by fear. More than any other emotion, fear has the ability to dictate how we live. If unchecked, fear will tell us everything from how to think to how to dress. Fear will keep us locked in our homes or make us run into the desert.

To be afraid is to live with a sense of constant dread waiting for another disaster to happen, the next killer bacteria to hit, or the bad news to come with the mail carrier. Fear is a kind of septic hydraulic fluid that fills us and turns us involuntarily whatsoever way it desires. To be afraid means that we focus on our nakedness and not on anything else, including God. Fear involves the expectation of punishment (see 1 Jn. 4:18). When I am afraid, I live to avoid consequences rather than to love and please God.

Alone

Are you afraid of the dark? I think that all of us at some time or another were or are afraid of the dark—or are we?

When our children woke up in the middle of the night from a bad dream or at the crack of a thunderstorm, they would cry out. I don't recall ever hearing any of my children crying out, "It's dark! It's dark!" More often than not they would cry out, "Mommy, Mommy," or "Daddy, Daddy." It was not just an absence of light in their bedrooms that made them afraid; it was being alone in the dark that was the source of fear. We are not afraid of the dark; we are afraid of being alone in the dark!

The greatest fear that we experience is not against some dire circumstance or threat; it is our fear of being alone. I recall a young man whom I'll call Jacob who came to us for ministry. Jacob had grown up in the church and seemed to be a cheerful and talented person, secure in all that he did. But there was another Jacob who few people knew.

When Jacob came to us for ministry, he seemed very unsettled. He came into the office looking around at everything as if searching for something. His face held a kind of nervous smile, but he was clearly not at ease. As we talked, it became evident that Jacob lived his life wrapped in incredible fear. He was unable to sit still and was bound by an astounding array of compulsive behaviors. And though he was a large man, Jacob felt threatened by almost everything and was never able to rest.

During our prayer ministry, the Lord led Jacob to a memory of hiding under his bed in the dark where he felt safe. These times of hiding usually followed some kind of perceived threat or upset. Many times they followed frightful apocalyptic sermons about the rapture. He seemed to be afraid of everything, including God. From childhood, Jacob heard sermons about an angry and vengeful God who was distant and difficult to please, a God of religious practice and unreachable standards of perfection. Relationship with this disinterested God seemed veiled behind insurmountable demands. Jacob was sure that after the rapture he would be left all *alone*.

As we prayed and asked God to reveal the truth about Jacob's fear, the Lord gave Jacob a picture of Jesus crawling under that bed to be with him and said, "You are not alone. I was with you under the bed and I will never leave you." Jacob experienced the truth of God's love as the presence of Jesus wrapped around him like a warm blanket in the darkness under his bed.

The truth broke the power of the lie, and now he is no longer alone and afraid in the dark.

Nervous, Paralyzed

Fear has the ability to rivet our attention and paralyze us just as it did Elijah, trapping him in the desert in fear. Fear has done its work in me personally many times, but perhaps never more than at my very first trumpet recital in college.

When I was a freshman music major at Saint Vincent College, I was asked to play in a student recital during my first semester. This was a rare and obvious privilege because freshmen seldom or never played in any solo or student recital. Those opportunities were reserved for upperclassmen. However, my teacher wanted me to play, and I agreed to perform a particularly difficult piece.

All was well with me; I had the piece down cold. I showed up at the recital wearing my best duds with my trumpet polished bright enough to blind even the most cynical stuffed shirt in the audience. I watched as the other students took the stage and created a silent running commentary in my head as to how each one fared and how thrilled the audience would react to my flawless performance. Then it was my turn.

The stage was set for my debut into collegiate musical history. They raised the lid of the grand piano so that the pianist could accompany the brilliant spectacle of my sound. With everything set, I strode out past the curtain and took center stage. Although the bright lights in the recital hall were shining in my eyes, I could still see that the hall was packed (not just for me, mind you, though I'm sure I thought so at the time.) As I looked out into the darkened sea of unfamiliar faces, my heart began to beat a little faster—then faster—then faster.

Suddenly I was filled with fear. My fingers couldn't find the valve buttons on my trumpet. My instrument, which just minutes ago had seemed like a natural extension of my body in the warm-up room, now seemed like a foreign object in my hands. It felt as though I was having one of those dreams when you appear naked in front of people. *What is this thing? How do you play it? What's the first note?!*

The piano began the first strains of introduction, and then it was time to attack the first note—but there was no spit in my mouth. The first note came, and I pressed the trumpet so hard to my mouth I thought my front teeth were loosened. Then it came. Sounds such as I had never heard began to plop from the end of my trumpet—as though someone had stuffed something in the end of my trumpet. My mouth felt like a cotton ball. I would have given a hundred dollars for some spit in my mouth, but there was none. It was a disaster of career-ending proportions.

After about ten minutes of cackling and hooting through my now ridiculously shiny instrument, the piece was mercifully over. I was so afraid that I forgot a repeat and totally missed a whole section of music. I was terrible—frozen—paralyzed. In short, I stank! The applause was brief and polite. I was humiliated and felt like saying, "Excuse me" on the way to find the nearest trash bin where I could toss my stupid trumpet. I hurried off the stage and away from my professor. Thank God, it was not my last recital, though I considered taking my trumpet instructor's advice to turn my trumpet into a decorative lamp and go to work in a steel mill.

Fear immobilizes us and keeps us from moving on into God's purposes for our lives. Fear is rooted in our lack of understanding our security in the love of God. As a result, we feel alone and destabilized by the slightest concern. We suffer from pain in the past, we feel paralysis in the present, and we are petrified of the future.

Cautious, Indecisive

Under the influence of fear, we live with a sense of dread and desperation. We walk through life taking short, cautious steps, suspicious of everyone and everything. We expect no grace from anyone and cannot afford to extend any either.

Fear causes us to live from one choppy, tentative step to the next. We are afraid to make a decision because we might make the wrong one. We are in fear of new relationships because we might get hurt. Therefore, whether it's a new relationship or a new revelation of God, we find it difficult to move ahead. Our tentative steps may be caused by the echo of a parent telling us we can't ever do anything right, so we don't do anything for fear of making mistakes. No decision seems safer than the wrong one. Whatever the source, fear becomes a drag on us that keeps us from enjoying life in all its fullness.

The fear that controls us today, with all its effects, is rooted in the past. It may be the result of a single painful event or the climate of a dysfunctional home. Much of our friend Jacob's fear in the present was rooted in the legalistic and graceless brand of religion that was a part of his early life. Jacob's fear was based on a wrong idea of God. He came to see God as far off and interested only in avenging every infraction of His stringent laws. Healing came when Jacob learned the truth that God had not and would not leave him alone. Neither will He leave any of us alone.

The Truth About Fear

So He said, "Go forth, and stand on the mountain before the Lord." And behold, the Lord was passing by! And a great and strong wind was rending the mountains and breaking in pieces the rocks before the Lord; but the Lord was not in the wind. And after the wind an earthquake, but the Lord was not in the earthquake. And after the earthquake a fire, but the Lord was not in the fire; and after the fire a sound of a gentle blowing. And it came about when Elijah heard it, that he wrapped his face in his mantle, and went out and stood in the entrance of the cave. And behold, a voice came to him and said, "What are you doing here, Elijah?" (1 Kings 19:11-13)

"I am alone…." The words fell limply from Elijah's mouth as the prophet of God sat in the cave on God's mountain. No sooner had the reverberation of his words left the cold walls of his hiding place than he heard the sound of a strong wind blowing past the mouth of the cave. The sound was deafening. Soon, however, the sound seemed to intensify, shaking the ground in an earthquake.

"Lord, is that You?" Elijah said in his raised, quivering voice. But no reply came forth. Then the earthquake was joined by a fire from Heaven, like the fire Elijah himself had called down only days before. "Is that You—Lord?!" Elijah's voice now raised to a shout. "Is that You?" Nothing. He put his hands over his ears to shut out the deafening sounds.

When the natural and supernatural disturbances were at their peak—when it seemed that it could not get any louder—a sound began to seep through the bluster. It was faint, but as definite as the sound of a single violin playing a high sustained note above the din of a full orchestra. The sound seemed to grow, not louder, but more prominent as it continued. Eventually it was transformed into a breathy whisper that seemed to distract all of Elijah's attention from the storm—so much so that it caused him to stand up, uncover his ears, and step into the mouth of the cave to hear it better. It was as if the storm of his inner turmoil was being engulfed—embraced—in softness. The sound, as it drowned out the storm, was like that sound he had heard a hundred mothers utter to their crying babies. It was as though Elijah heard the sound of God's voice gently whispering, "Shhhhhh, Elijah. It will be okay. I am here…I am here…Shhhhhhh."

We Are Not Alone

As Elijah sat alone and afraid in the wilderness, the strong hands of a faithful and loving Father picked him up as one would a crying child and lifted him to His heart. Then, as Elijah was hiding in the cave, God answered his fear. God sent the strong wind, earthquake, and fire as signs of the inner turmoil of Elijah's heart—the result of fear that had blocked his view of God. But God was not in any of these. Once the fear of Elijah's heart was stirred, God sent the "sound of a gentle blowing" (1 Kings 19:12) to Elijah—the same sound that your mother or father made to quiet you when you woke up afraid and alone in the dark. It's a sound of comfort that God speaks to us in those places of darkness and fear: "Shhh, it's okay—everything will be all right. Daddy's here now. Don't be afraid."

When we run as far and hard as we can, we learn that the presence of God is already ahead of us and ready to pour out His mercy and grace. It was not a surprise that Elijah ran. God knew he was afraid. When Elijah reached the middle of the wilderness, he was met by the mercy of God in the form of a shade tree under which God provided an angel with food and water. Elijah was not left alone in his fear.

When God picked up Elijah as a father would pick up a crying child and took him to His heart, Elijah's complaint—the source of his fear—was in his statement, "I am alone." The truth was and is that we are not alone, no matter what the circumstance.

God, through His representatives, tells us more than 300 times in the Scriptures not to be afraid. There is a "fear not" for every day of the year and every kind of circumstance we encounter. There was a "fear not" before Israel entered into the Promised Land. There was a "fear not" before God used Gideon to deliver Israel from the enemy. There was a "fear not" before Jesus was implanted by the Spirit in the womb of Mary. Throughout the Bible these "fear nots" came to assure those who received them that God's presence was with them even in the midst of great change or challenge. It was their assurance that God would not leave them alone in the dark.

The assurance of God's presence was given to the nation of Israel many times when they faced the possibility of danger. As they crossed the frontiers of promise God told them, "The Lord is the one who goes ahead of you; He will be with you. He will not fail you or forsake you. Do not fear or be dismayed" (Deut. 31:8), and "Have I not commanded you? Be strong and courageous! Do not tremble or be dismayed, for the Lord your God is with you wherever you go" (Josh. 1:9). When Israel was taken into captivity, God assured them that even in that place they were not alone. " 'But as for you, O Jacob My servant, do not fear, nor be dismayed, O Israel! For, see, I am going to save you from afar, and your descendants from the land of their captivity; and Jacob will return and be undisturbed and secure, with no one making him tremble. O Jacob My servant, do not fear,' declares the Lord, 'For I am with you' " (Jer. 46:27-28a).

Here the Lord makes a connection between our fears and His presence. God's strategy to protect or heal us from fear is to tell us that He is "with us." Many times in our ministry I have heard people who lived in fear say that they were alone in a time of abuse. Invariably God brought healing to them by showing them in some way that He was, in fact, always there with them and that they were never alone. Somehow the light of God's presence with them dispelled the fear that had controlled them, in some cases, for decades.

Being healed from a controlling fear is a matter of recognizing and appropriating the presence of God whether in the present or in the context of past memories. In order to deal with the issue of fear, we must trace it to its root in our own past and allow the presence of God to debunk the lie that we were alone in our fear. We are not beyond God's presence in any place or any time. God will manifest His healing presence in our past just as He did when He showed Himself to that little boy under the bed. Again, we cannot change the event that caused the fear; that is history. But when we recognize that God did not leave us alone, the destructive and controlling influence of fear is destroyed.

Christ Was Alone So We Would Never Be

God the Father, knowing that the fear of being alone was the greatest issue, sent His Son Jesus to be "with us" and heal us of controlling fear. As the Gospel of Matthew says, " 'Behold, the virgin shall be with child and shall bear a Son, and they shall call His name Immanuel,' which translated means, 'God with us' " (Mt. 1:23). Jesus took all our fear and aloneness to the cross and was Himself alone and forsaken by the Father for a moment so that you and I would never fear being alone again (see Mt. 27:46).

God will meet you in your fear: past, present, and future. When you are afraid, God will meet you and speak to your heart, saying, "Shhh, I am here, and everything is okay. Don't be afraid." It is a sound that will cut through your strongest fear.

(See the *Personal Ministry Guide* at the end of this book to process the issue of fear.)

CHAPTER NINE

WHAT IS YOUR NAME?

Rejection

When He got out of the boat, immediately a man from the tombs with an unclean spirit met Him, and he had his dwelling among the tombs. And no one was able to bind him anymore, even with a chain; because he had often been bound with shackles and chains, and the chains had been torn apart by him and the shackles broken in pieces, and no one was strong enough to subdue him. Constantly, night and day, he was screaming among the tombs and in the mountains, and gashing himself with stones (Mark 5:2-5).

And when He came out onto the land, He was met by a man from the city who was possessed with demons; and who had not put on any clothing for a long time, and was not living in a house, but in the tombs (Luke 8:27).

The Portrait of Rejection

An unnamed man roams through the darkness in the place of the dead as if searching for something on the tomb markers, his jagged restlessness punctuated only by the cries of his mournful displacement. His unsteady hands grope from tomb to tomb, as he feels the sharpness of cold stones bruising his unshod feet. A shiver as lifeless as the moon that illuminates his staggering, gnome-like figure cuts through his uncovered body, reminding him that he has been abandoned to the dead—alone in his own body.

Jangling remnants of chains and shackles cut deeply into his flesh, increasing his torment with each movement. An aching emptiness surrounds him, and he cuts himself with the flinty edges of sharp stones as if to focus a pain that defies description. His anger rivals that of a wild animal whose life has been held in captivity—pitiful and unprotected in a place of deafening silence.

Then, with the first rays of dawn's light at his back, he spots a boat drifting toward the shore of the small sea by which he lives. *Why would a fishing boat come in with the last minutes of darkness? Fishing boats go out in the morning; they don't come in.* The recluse tightly squints his eyes to see who could be encroaching upon his exile among the dead. As he watches, the small, plain vessel floats to shore off a sea as still and as smooth as glass, its bow coming to gently rest on the dry land.

Something within the man from the tombs at once becomes unsettled—bereft of its security. At the same time there is something magnetic about the otherwise unexceptional figure who is stepping out of the boat across its bow. As the man from the boat approaches, the morning light from behind the anonymous wanderer's back begins to reveal the face of the man from the boat. All that is within the roaming man senses a presence he has longed to feel—an antidote for his disincorporation—a something to fill his nothingness. The demonic lies that bind him begin to tremble at the appearance of the Son of the Most High.

The Influence of Rejection

The lie believed by those who live under rejection is, "*I do not belong.*" They ask, "Who am I? Where do I belong? How do I fit in?" Someone lives under the influence of rejection when he wanders through life in an unsettled state never finding the place of rest. The man from the tombs lived in the *Gergasenes*, the other side of the sea from where Jesus lived. This was the place of the *Girgashites*. Both words stem from the Hebrew root *ger*, which is the word for a sojourner or stranger. Many people live their lives under this influence. They live like those who hung out on the periphery of the camp of Israel as outsiders. They are the *rejected*.

Rejection is a daily fact of life. When I was a kid, we played baseball almost every day. The kids in my neighborhood would hang their baseball mitts over their bicycle handlebars and converge on the nearest field or schoolyard any day there was no school and whenever there was no snow on the ground. When we could recruit enough players, two captains would toss a baseball bat back and forth in a ritual that would decide who got the first pick of the other kids to be on their teams. One after the other, players were selected from the most athletic to the least. The greatest fear was to be selected last or perhaps not at all. As the lines of available players grew shorter, those still remaining sank into a kind of resignation of "lastness." That feeling of being last—of being somehow less acceptable or desirable than others—left an impression on those at the end of the line. Many times I was one of those.

We all experience rejection simply because we are not good at everything. A person selected first in a pick-up game may be the last one chosen for the debate team or the last person you would want to balance your checkbook. Many people today wander from one line to the next, hoping to be placed higher in the order than the last line they found themselves in. Those who live in such rejection say to themselves, "I am not acceptable…I do not belong…I don't fit in…" or words to that effect. They are the kids in school who are taller, shorter, fatter, thinner, or just different. The key word here is *different*.

Rejection is the result of an imperfect or conditional love. It is a love that says, "I will love you if you are worth it to me." This imperfect love leads to great fear of not being accepted by others. Why is this such an issue? God created us to live in community, and He said that it is not good for us to be alone (see Gen. 2:18). Community, belonging to one another, is a strong instinct within us. We are created in community, reflecting the very schematic of God Himself, who exists as a community of sorts: Father, Son, and Holy Spirit. Thus we all were made for each other. If we do not experience that belonging, we wither and die.

Those who feel rejection are those who live in the cold outer darkness on the fringes of the camp, existing on the scraps of attention thrown to them by the people closer to the fire—by those who seem to be less *different* than they.

The tomb wanderer is a picture of someone who lives in rejection. We don't know what is responsible for his unfortunate state, but he seems typical of others who find themselves on the outside looking in, trying to discover who they are and where they fit in.

There are several aspects in this picture that describe those who live under the influence of rejection. I will interpret these passages of Scripture in a very literal way as a conversation between Jesus and one rejected man, who exemplifies many others living under the influence of rejection.

Emotional Profile of Rejection

The influence of rejection creates its own emotional profile. Here are a few ways the rejected feel.

Separated, Left Out

Many people who suffer under the influence of rejection live in a state of separation. The man from the tombs had placed himself where no other person would enter—among the dead. Dead bodies were considered to be unclean and a source of possible defilement to Jewish people. Yet, it seems as though the tomb wanderer himself was Jewish because he called Jesus the "Son of the Most High," a term not likely to be used by someone outside the nation of Israel.

Those who live under the influence of rejection tend to pull away from others to avoid being rejected again. They position themselves in places of unavailability, out of the reach of others, and do so in several different ways. For example, they may separate themselves by building a façade of legalism or piety so as to seem unapproachable. No matter how they pull away, though, they are like the tomb wanderer who placed himself out of the range of others.

Confused

As I stated earlier, I want to interpret this passage in a literal rather than a spiritual way. The man among the tombs was said to have an "unclean spirit." The Greek word used is *akathartos*, which may be interpreted as a polluted spirit. There is a sort of confusion that surrounds the rejected. Their spirits are polluted as they try to find acceptance. Imagine the kind of traffic jam that went on in the tomb wanderer's head. Hundreds of voices vied for attention and comfort at the same time. He walked about in a confused state, not knowing who or what he was.

We pollute our spirits in many ways by willfully taking on new strategies and disguises to hide our pain. But whatever we take onto ourselves to gain acceptance—other than our acceptance in Christ—will never work. Instead these things will become the source of pollution in our own spirits and rob us of true intimacy with God.

Nameless

Rejected people struggle with identity. It is *who* they are that is being denied. This is illustrated as the man wandered among the tombs without a robe (see Lk. 8:27). The outer robe, or *himation*, was a distinguishing garment bearing the identity of a family. More than an article of clothing, this robe provided a sense of security to the wearer. He lived in it, worked in it, slept in it. It was his life. The fact that the man had no robe demonstrated a lack of identity and security. Without it, as without the unconditional acceptance that we all need, the man lived a cold and anonymous life.

People who live with rejection take on various disguises to gain some kind of acceptable identity. In my younger years I took on the disguise of a "cool musician." When I was very young, my parents noticed that I could whistle a tune or remember a melody sung on a TV commercial. When one of my older brothers left for the Marines in the early 1960's, I borrowed his beaten-up, old cornet and taught myself to play a little, which got the attention of family and friends. Throughout my school years and long after, I was driven to play music. It became my whole life—the thing I was betting on to keep me out of the darkness and oblivious to rejection. I was a trumpet player. I was fairly good at it and began to play professionally when I was just 15 years old, alongside guys who were in their 20's and 30's or older. It made me feel like I was somebody. But behind the music there was a frightened, rejected kid who just wanted someone to notice he was there. In the end, I was able to make a living playing the trumpet, though it drew me further into isolation and away from God and people.

An individual's identity may be denied in many ways. Perhaps overbearing parents control every aspect of a child's life to the point that it crushes his or her sense of identity, leaving the child no room to grow. Or it can also happen if a child has too little attention from his parents. Children may feel rejected when their parents try to live their lives over again through them, thereby denying their offspring individuality and identity.

Maybe this is why we see children and young adults wearing rings in every body part that can be pierced, dyeing their hair purple, or straining to keep up with the latest styles. They want someone to notice them—to accept them as individuals. They, like the tomb wanderer, are yearning for a way to belong, a way to blend into the crowd, a way to stay close to the fire.

Angry

Rejection, remember, is the result of imperfect love. Love that is imperfect holds some kind of condition or criteria for acceptance. It is a love that makes us conform to someone's arbitrary standard. The man from the tombs had been shackled and chained many times—only to break free and wander off again. Those shackles and chains were an attempt to control how he walked or lived. Probably some well-meaning folks thought that this man's problems could be taken care of if he would just "live like us." Those restraints, however, only served to make him feel more rejected—more angry.

His breaking free of those chains and shackles in such great ferocity is a demonstration of anger, which is a big part of rejection. The Bible unfolds a pattern of rejection that leads to anger that in turn leads to death. Cain believed God rejected him, and he became angry and murdered his brother Abel (see Gen. 4:1-8). Esau, deprived of his father's blessing, felt rejected and wanted to kill his brother Jacob (see Gen. 27:34-41). God rejected Saul for his disobedience (see 1 Sam. 15:26), and Saul spent the last years of his life chasing David, God's anointed one, to kill him (see 1 Sam. 19:1; 20:31). Where there is rejection, there is anger and death.

I have noticed in the Bible and in our ministry that such anger is usually pointed at someone whom we feel is more accepted than we are. Tragically, this is probably true of those children who walk into school with guns to blow away those who are the more accepted kids—the cool kids.

For example, kids who were angry and felt rejected, populated the "Trench Coat Mafia" of Columbine High School in Littleton, Colorado. Eventually, two of them acted out their rejection. They made lists of other students whom they saw as more accepted and systematically sought them out to murder them. *Rejection* led to *anger* that led to *death*.

Restless, Unsettled

The man from the tombs was a man crying out "night and day," which is a way of saying that he had no rest. His crying and screaming were like the cries and howls of a wounded animal calling attention to its pain. Though we have no recording of the words he cried out, his message is clear: "Does anyone see me? Does anyone care?"

The man also gashed himself with sharp stones to increase the volume and intensity of his call, much like the prophets of Baal whose god did not hear them (see 1 Kings 18:28). Those living outside the warmth and glow of the campfire are calling out to be noticed—to be called closer to the fire. They feel forgotten and forsaken. We have ministered many times to the rejected who have harmed themselves in some way. Sometimes they cut themselves; sometimes they starve themselves. The self-hurt seems to be a way for them to be able to cry out louder, for those who feel rejected also feel unheard. They are crying out to belong—to feel a part of something warm and loving.

The Truth About Rejection

And seeing Jesus from a distance, he ran up and bowed down before Him; and crying out with a loud voice, he said, "What do I have to do with You, Jesus, Son of the Most High God? I implore You by God, do not torment me!" For He had been saying to him, "Come out of the man, you unclean spirit!" And He was asking him, "What is your name?" And he said to Him, "My name is Legion; for we are many." And he began to entreat Him earnestly not to send them out of the country. Now there was a big herd of swine feeding there on the mountain. And the demons entreated Him, saying, "Send us into the swine so that we may enter them." And He gave them permission. And coming out, the un-clean spirits entered the swine; and the herd rushed down the steep bank into the sea, about two thousand of them; and they were drowned in the sea. And their herdsmen ran away and reported it in the city and out in the country. And the people came to see what it was that had happened. And they came to Jesus and ob-served the man who had been demon-possessed sitting down, clothed and in his right mind, the very man who had had the "legion"; and they became frightened (Mark 5:6-15).

A thousand episodes of emptiness flooded the tomb wan-derer's memory. As the illumined figure from the boat stood be-fore him, the wanderer threw himself at Jesus' feet. A voice rose up out of the loneliness of the man's heart, shattering the silence between them and giving expression to the pain in the wander-er's heart. "What do we have to do with one another—who are You—who am I? Don't torment me anymore—don't play games with me, Son of the Most High. Don't give me another ser-mon…I don't need three steps to acceptability. I need to be warm—to be close. I need to know, do You accept me? Do You have a place for me?"[1]

Now, in this most pregnant moment, a gentle voice issued from the mouth of the Man from the boat, His words striking deep into the heart of the solitary man from the tombs: "What is your name?" The question reverberated in the man's mind, stirring a thousand voices wanting to respond. "I am a legion of names—I have tried everything to get close." But now, looking up into the face of Jesus, the tomb wanderer's heart became still—just as the sea had done only hours earlier at the voice of Jesus (see Mk. 4:35-41). The question and the answer both issued from the same mouth.

Jesus had come to the place of this man's darkness and rejection. It was for *him* that Jesus left His home. It was for *him* that Jesus fought seas, conquered storms, and brought peace. It was for *him* that Jesus sailed through the darkness to this lonely desolate place of the dead. There could be no stronger words of acceptance.

With his eyes full of the face of Jesus, words were not needed. In His coming, Jesus had answered the man's desperate inquiry, "Who am I? Who are You?" Implicitly Jesus was saying, "You are the one I have come for—for you! You belong to Me! That is who you are. Here is where you belong!"

---

1. Note that my interpretation of this passage is very literal. The man was obviously filled with demonic presence but they all spoke through the man's mouth. I am interpreting in a way that shows the response of those living under the influence of rejection, not to in any way deny the demonic that was so apparently present in the man. A careful reading of the text indicates that Jesus was speaking to the man and that the demons answered through the man's mouth. Note the use of the masculine singular in the text. The "*he*" in verse 7 is the man.

    "Seeing Jesus from a distance, **he** *ran up and bowed down before Him; and shouting with a loud voice,* **he** *said, 'What business do we have with each other, Jesus, Son of the Most High God? I implore You by God, do not torment* **me** *!' For He had been saying to* **him** *, 'Come out of the man, you unclean spirit!' And He was asking* **him** *, 'What is* **your** *name?' And* **he** *said to Him, '* **My** *name is Legion; for we are many' "* (Mk. 5:6-9).

With that gesture, Jesus walked up to every wallflower who had ever been, or ever would be, and said, "Who are *you*? I want to know *you*—yes, *you*!"

With the truth declared, the demons inside the man—his many ideas about himself and his attempts to find acceptance—had to flee to the nearest swine. Once truth comes and the lies are displaced, the forces of hell have no legal place to stand and must therefore go. And they went!

The truth now announced for the world to hear, the man's restless wandering ceased. His friends found this formerly tormented man sitting down, no longer wandering. He was wearing a new robe, clothed with the name of the One who came just for him, and able to truthfully relate to God and the world. He was in his right mind—he had a new revelation of who he was in the face of Jesus Christ (see Mk. 5:15).

We Are Accepted in Christ

There is no night too dark, no shore too distant, for the presence and compassion of God. There was no other purpose for Jesus on that shore that day; no other ministry event was recorded in that place. Jesus came just for this man to bring him to Himself. The simple truth about rejection that we have heard uttered time and time again in ministry sessions is that we are who we are in Christ Jesus. We are defined and identified solely by our relationship with Him. We are who He says we are, not who the world says we are.

It is impossible for God to forget us or to ignore us. As the prophet says, "Remember these things, O Jacob, and Israel, for you are My servant; I have formed you, you are My servant, O Israel, you will not be forgotten by Me" (Is. 44:21). To those of you who have lived on the edge of the camp, in the outer cold away from the fire, God has brought the fire to you. You are no longer outsiders, but the ultimate insiders—inside the heart of God.

The psalmist writes prophetically of Jesus, who would suffer the ultimate rejection and injustice of the cross:

My God, my God, why have You forsaken me? Far from my deliverance are the words of my groaning. O my

God, I cry by day, but You do not answer; and by night, but I have no rest (Psalm 22:1-2).

It was Christ who was forsaken; the Father's back was to Him. It was Jesus who groaned in the pain of utter aloneness and separation from the Father. It was Jesus who cried out in the pain of rejection so that we would not have to. It was Jesus who knew the unrelenting torment and restless condition of the cross so that you and I would be able to rest in His finished work. It was Jesus who was despised and rejected of men who hid their faces from Him (see Is. 53:3).

We are made acceptable by the blood of Jesus alone. "He saved us, not on the basis of deeds which we have done in righteousness, but according to His mercy" (Tit. 3:5a). We have been "accepted in the beloved [Jesus]" (Eph. 1:6 KJV). It is an acceptance that is incorruptible and unconditional. No one can take it away from us, and it will never be out of style.

In our acceptance we can now risk the company of others who may or may not accept us. The man among the tombs to whom Jesus had taken this message of acceptance wanted to jump into the boat with Jesus to follow Him. Jesus instructed him, however, to go back home—probably to the very ones who rejected him—to bring word of God's goodness to him. The man did as Jesus instructed and those who saw him and knew him were amazed at the mercy of God. We are accepted by the Lord Jesus who has come for us, and out of that acceptance we can accept others.

Our Identity Is in Christ

What is your name? Who are you? Where do you belong? Jesus gives us a new identity and therefore a new and incorruptible acceptance. It is possible that others may have turned their backs on us, but Jesus stands with arms open wide to receive us. Jesus has set sail to reach the rejected—He has calmed the raging sea and sailed through the darkness just for you. He left His own comfort and crossed a storm-tossed blackness to walk right into our rejection so that we could be healed by His presence.

As you read these very words, know that the living and ascended Christ has come for you. The boat has set sail. He has calmed the sea and has come for you. Who He says you are is who you are!

(See the *Personal Ministry Guide* at the end of this book to process the issue of rejection.)

CHAPTER TEN

LIVING IN SECOND PLACE

Worthlessness

Now Laban had two daughters: Leah, who was the oldest, and her younger sister, Rachel. Leah had pretty eyes, but Rachel was beautiful in every way, with a lovely face and shapely figure (Genesis 29:16-17 NLT).

The Portrait of Worthlessness

She had pretty eyes. She was a pleasant and mature young woman, and as the older daughter of Laban, Leah prepared to assume the responsibility of running a household. She was accountable for her younger sister Rachel from the time she was an infant, and she learned everything there was to know about maintaining home and family. Leah had ripened on the vine of Laban's house and was the best that Laban had to offer.

Then one day, Jacob came into her father's house. He was a handsome and talented man, and everything he touched seemed to turn to gold. He was an infusion of new blood into the family, and it seemed natural to everyone that a merger should take place between the house of Laban and the grandson of Abraham. And what better way to bring the two houses together than through the union of Laban's oldest daughter and the son of Isaac? It just made sense.

The oldest daughter of Laban was thrilled at the prospect of marriage. The preparations were made and the invitations sent. Like any other girl of her time, she dreamed of setting up her own home and raising her own family. The day had been fixed for the wedding feast, and she began to make preparations for a new life.

When the day of building her own house had come, the feast was loud and joyous, and the whole neighborhood showed up. All her friends and family were there as well to witness the joining of the two houses. The food and the celebration seemed endless, and everyone had a great time. When the celebration was over, Leah was brought to the tent where her marriage with Jacob would be consummated. She wore a veil that covered her from head to toe, obscuring not only her pretty eyes but also her form. The time had come—a new era had begun in her life.

Then came…the morning after. The party was over, and only the stillness and grog of the next day remained. As she awakened, the sleepy but contented bride looked over into the face of her husband, thrilled with the prospect of married life. As her husband awoke, he slowly looked back into her pretty eyes. But his air of delight quickly vanished as surprise and betrayal filled his face. His eyes opened wider with disbelief. Sitting up suddenly, Jacob quickly grabbed something to cover himself and sprang from his bed. "What's this? What are you doing here? You were not the one I wanted, not the one I worked for!"

Considered a disappointment—less than he expected— worth less than her sister, Leah was thrust into a place that she had never planned and didn't deserve—a life of second place.

The Lie of Worthlessness

Think about it for a minute. How would you feel if you woke up on the day after your wedding and your spouse declared that you were a disappointment, that he or she wanted someone else—even your own sibling? Such was the case for Leah, who lived under the influence of worthlessness. The lie of worthlessness is "*I am not as good*"—that our worth is determined by comparison to someone else. A person lives under the influence of worthlessness when he or she tries to work and perform their way to approval, as Leah did. We see ourselves in terms of everybody else, and we spend our lives chasing some kind of ideal that doesn't exist anywhere but in the heads of those who feel worth less.

Worthlessness is the influence of the *Amorites*. The root of the name Amorite comes from the word that means to speak or declare something. In this case we are referring to things spoken over us that do not agree with the purpose or the promises of

God. It was the Amorites who opposed the progression of God's people into the land of promise. They stood against the nation of Israel and the Word of God (see Num. 21:21-35). The lie of worthlessness declares that we are worth less than God has declared. Those who live under the influence of worthlessness feel devalued as they compare themselves to other people.

The world, and dare I say even the Church, has created a prototype of perfection that makes us feel guilty for not looking like the people on magazine covers. We are compared to the tall, the rich, the smart—the prom queens and football captains. Everyone should be young, white, thin, rich...you name it. If we don't conform, we become invisible and unimportant to those who compare more favorably, or who at least think they do.

Anyone who does not adapt to the prototype is dismissed to the nerd table in the cafeteria. They are like the rest of the wolves in the pack who live below the Alpha, or dominant, pair. In truth, most of us are somewhere down the alphabet from the Alphas of the world. We are not wolves, but we live like them, ready to snarl our disapproval of those on the fringes of the pack. Yes, there is a trend even among the saints of God to value others by the kind of car they park in the parking lot on Sunday morning or by the amount of tithe they bring.

Life in second place has its destructive and limiting effects on us. As we look at Leah's life, a picture emerges that describes the Betas (those who believe they are in second place) who live in lesser places—who feel worth *less* than the Alphas of the world.

Leah had weak or "pretty eyes," as the New Living Translation states. She didn't have the dark, passionate eyes that were so admired among the ancient Middle Eastern people. She didn't stand out alongside her sister, who was said to be beautiful in form and figure. She was just an average person, like most of us. Many today who live under this influence of comparison spend their lives trying to achieve that magazine cover perfection.

The truth is that most of us are average and will not appear any time soon on a movie screen, yet we still look to the world for approval that is, at best, fleeting. That approval will disappear along with our hair and youthful form. Whatever appeals to the world will sag or wear out sooner or later. Worldly approval passes swiftly, and it is that which is truly worthless.

As we look at Leah's life, a picture emerges of those who believe they are worthless. Even the names Leah gave to her children demonstrate something of how she felt. Taken together, they present a vivid portrait of those who believe themselves to be worth less than someone else.

Emotional Profile of Worthlessness

Those who live under the influence of worthlessness feel like Leah felt. They believe they are unloved.

Unloved

The first and greatest effect of the lie of worthlessness is the belief that we are unloved, or perhaps more accurately, that we are loved *less*. In some sense, we believe that we are less lovable than someone else. Leah believed that her first two sons were God's response to the fact that she was unloved.

> *Now the Lord saw that Leah was **unloved**, and He opened her womb, but Rachel was barren. Leah conceived and bore a son and named him Reuben, for she said, "Because the Lord has seen my affliction; surely now my husband will love me." Then she conceived again and bore a son and said, "Because the Lord has heard that I am unloved, He has therefore given me this son also." So she named him Simeon* (Genesis 29:31-33, emphasis added).

It was not that Leah was not loved, but that she was not loved the same way her sister was loved. She was the good and responsible daughter of Laban. She was like the girl whom everyone wants as friend in study hall but would not ask to the prom. It wasn't that Leah was not loved, but that she was not the love of someone's life. She was not special.

Unnoticed

The names of her first two sons, Reuben and Simeon, describe her feelings of being ignored—*unnoticed*. Leah declared that in giving birth to her first son Reuben (meaning, "see a son," or perhaps "you see a son"), God had seen her "affliction" or humiliation. Imagine how Leah must have felt seeing her husband go into the tent of her younger sister, the one she helped to raise.

Leah's second son, Simeon, whose name comes from the word for hearing, adds to her belief that no one noticed her for who she was—no one but God, that is. Those who live under the influence of this lie of worthlessness live a life in the shadows of the beautiful people. They are like the girl who stands alongside the head cheerleader, unnoticed. The Leahs of the world are the ones who do their jobs and seldom complain. They believe themselves to be ordinary, unexceptional people.

Unattached

Realizing that the birth of two sons did not buy any self-worth for Leah, she placed her hope in another son—Levi.

> *She conceived again and bore a son and said, "Now this time my husband will become attached to me, because I have borne him three sons." Therefore he was named Levi* (Genesis 29:34).

We are created to feel attached to other humans; we have a designed need for connectedness. Subsequently, there is a sense of emptiness when we don't experience the kind of emotional heart attachment we need. Leah tried to perform her way into an emotional bond with Jacob.

Leah's son's name, Levi, could be interpreted as "my attachment." Having another son was her ticket to the warmth of her husband. Leah, like others who live under the influence of worthlessness, experienced conditional love in her connection to other people. Such individuals feel that they must do something to earn that love, whether it's hitting a baseball for Dad or scoring 1400 on SAT tests. They are not worth the love in themselves.

Then, Leah had a fourth son, Judah. With the birth of this son she felt free to praise Jehovah. She declared, "This time I will praise the Lord" (Gen. 29:35). This time she shifted to the means by which she gained attachment. I have heard people many times being praised or approved for some physical aspect of beauty or some "anointing" they are perceived to have. Although this sounds like genuine praise, it is once again conditioned on something.

Jealous

Those who don't experience the intimacy of affection and approval look with longing and envy at those who do. The biblical text indicates that Leah believed that Jacob was her husband and that Rachel stole him. When Rachel asked for the mandrake roots gathered by Leah's son, Leah replied, "Is it a small matter for you to take my husband?" (Gen. 30:15) Her question to Rachel not only verifies that she believed herself to be the intended wife of Jacob, but also points out that those who believe they are worth less tend to be jealous of those who have more.

Those who live under worthlessness spend their time looking to see who got the bigger piece of the pie. The result is that they seldom are satisfied with the piece of the pie they have. They don't see that sometimes those who get the bigger slice also get a stomachache. They grow weary in comparison and are never satisfied even in their relationship with God. Someone will always be smarter, prettier, taller, or thinner—there will always be someone to envy.

Unworthy

People who don't feel they compare well with others spend their time trying to prove their worth. Leah's name means "wearied." The name fits, because she spent her life trying to prove her worth to her husband by having children.

The name and the account of Issachar's birth give us a picture of love bought. Leah actually purchased the love and affections of her husband with a few mandrake roots. She said to Jacob, "You must come in to me, for I have surely hired you with my son's mandrakes" (Gen. 30:16). Leah believed that she had to purchase the love of her husband.

Others of us may not purchase a night in the honeymoon suite with mandrake roots, but we still pay for the love and acceptance of other people. We may pay this bill by endless activity or works done to get noticed or feel worthwhile. But eventually morning will come and Jacob will get up and go back to Rachel's tent. At the end of the day we will still feel empty—unworthy.

Unapproved

With the birth of Zebulun, Leah proclaimed that she had now presented a sufficient dowry for her husband. Bear in mind that she herself had already given Jacob five sons and two more by her servant. But no matter what she did, she still lacked a sense of final approval and acceptance from her husband. This seems to sum up the belief of those under the influence of worthlessness: No matter what they do, no matter how hard they try, they never find approval.

Carolyn was a vibrant, youthful woman in her mid-40's who, despite her great love of God and her many gifts for ministry and personal affability, never seemed to be able to come to the point of satisfaction with her life. She was tormented by the feeling that she could never do enough things or do them well enough. This seemed to go against common sense and appearances because she was first at everything. She was a homecoming queen and a top student—one of the "Alphas" of the world. But somehow she was still empty. Carolyn came from a strong Christian family and her father was a career military man. She had always earned good grades and did what good girls do; but nothing she did ever satisfied her.

As we prayed together, the Lord allowed her to remember a time when she was in her late 20's, playing on a women's competitive softball league. She was a good athlete who had a strong love for the Lord and for her family. In this memory frame, Carolyn was playing in a game when she got a good hit that came at a crucial time in the game. When the girl who followed her in the batting order also got a hit, Carolyn scored a run. It was all very exciting.

The first thing that Carolyn wanted to do when she crossed home plate was to go into the stands to find her father, who had come to see her play in the game. She found him sitting behind the dugout and ran over to him excited about what she had done. He was smiling and happy to see her, but when she got next to him, he said something like, "Well, Peanut, if you would have widened your batting stance a little, you might have gotten a better hit." She was crushed like a beach ball run over by a truck. She had not come to him for batting tips; she wanted his approval and affection and for him to share in her excitement.

It was clear that Carolyn believed that no matter what she did in any area of life, it would never be as good as what someone else did. She would never find approval. She had lived under the influence of the lie of worthlessness. As we continued to pray, we asked the Lord Himself to reveal the truth to her. Immediately, the image of a picture came to mind with Jesus standing behind a small child at home plate in a baseball game. Jesus was smiling in the picture, just enjoying being with the child. The child had not accomplished anything yet. He was simply standing at the plate!

The message was clear: The Lord was pleased with the child and with Carolyn regardless of how well she did something. His hands were on the bat with hers, and He was having fun and enjoying her. The lie of worthlessness was deflated as her ego had been a few moments earlier. We praised God and wept for His love toward her as His special child.

The Truth About Worthlessness

We Are God's Workmanship

The truth regarding the lie of worthlessness is that there is no second place. God does not compare us with any other person. We are handmade originals. We are not cheap, mass-produced fiddles from the wholesale house; we are Stradivarius violins, priceless and incomparable even to another Stradivarius. Have you heard of these violins? *Antonius* Stradivarius made what are now the hallmark of all violins in the 1600 and 1700s. Even now, hundreds of years later, they are still considered to be the greatest ever built.

As far as I know, there has never been a second-rate Stradivarius violin. Each original that was ever made by maestro Stradivarius' hand had a quality of its own. He handpicked the wood for each one, and the oil of his own hands was impregnated in the aged wooden parts. The sound was unique in each instrument, and each one sang out the praise of its maker.

In the same way, the only comparison we can make of ourselves among others is that we are incomparable to any other person ever made. We are as original and unique as our fingerprints.

The Word of God is clear on who made us:

Know that the Lord Himself is God; it is He who has made us, and not we ourselves; we are His people and the sheep of His pasture. Enter His gates with thanksgiving and His courts with praise. Give thanks to Him, bless His name. For the Lord is good; His lovingkindness is everlasting and His faithfulness to all generations (Psalm 100:3-5).

For You formed my inward parts; You wove me in my mother's womb. I will give thanks to You, for I am fearfully and wonderfully made; wonderful are Your works, and my soul knows it very well (Psalm 139:13-14).

Thus says the Lord, your Redeemer, and the one who formed you from the womb, "I, the Lord, am the maker of all things" (Isaiah 44:24a).

For we are His workmanship, created in Christ Jesus for good works, which God prepared beforehand so that we would walk in them (Ephesians 2:10).

As God's irreplaceable and handmade creations, we cannot be compared to any other. We belong to Him.

We Are Precious

Each of us is a special creation of God. What is important to God seldom appears important to man. God does not see things in the carnal comparative way that we do, any more than we see our own children in that way.

Although both Leah and Rachel bore children who were important to the nation of Israel, it was Leah who brought forth the firstborn son of Jacob, Reuben, and it was from her son Judah that the Messiah of the world would descend. It was from Leah that the Levitical priesthood would spring forth. And finally, it was Leah who was buried alongside her husband, not Rachel (see Gen. 49:29-33).

God Does Not Compare Us

"...God sees not as man sees, for man looks at the outward appearance, but the Lord looks at the heart" (1 Samuel 16:7).

God is not concerned about the world's opinion or judgment of us. The Lord does not always use the people who are the most talented, beautiful, or gifted; rather, He uses those people in whom He has developed character. Think about Leah, Moses, David, and Jesus. In fact, Jesus was nothing special in appearance; He was an average-looking Joshua (see Is. 53:2).

God is more concerned with the heart. Leah had a heart to fear the Lord. She was not party to the superstition of her father's idols as Rachel was, who stole them (see Gen. 31:19). It was Leah, the one with the pretty eyes, who loved the Lord.

The Picture of Truth

The truth about worthlessness is summed up in a picture that arose during a ministry session with Corrine. Corrine was the middle one of three sisters, each one beautiful and talented in her own way. And though they loved one another, they also were always comparing themselves to one another.

Corrine was also the divorced mother of three children. She described to me her life of busyness and activity, but it was one in which she felt no true satisfaction. She was involved in everything, yet never felt she could do enough. Though she was obviously an attractive woman, she constantly compared herself to both her sisters, finding ways they were better or more worth-while than she. In addition, she compared her appearance and her education to that of her siblings and arrived at the opinion that she really "had nothing to offer."

When the lie of worthlessness was uncovered, the Lord walked her to a memory picture of sitting on the bed behind her older sister, watching the sister brush her own hair. She could see the smiling, lovely face of her sister, but she could not see her own face. She was invisible even to herself. The lie she believed was that she had nothing to offer—that she was just the middle and unexceptional sister. When she herself spoke the lie, I asked the Lord to manifest the truth to her. I had not even finished my sentence before the Lord gave her an image of Him standing be-hind her and brushing her hair. This was the Lord's way of say-ing, "You are precious and special to Me." Tears came with the truth, as they usually do. Corrine was special—she was the one whose hair was brushed by the Lord Himself. What could be clearer?

The truth is that we are God's creation—His own children. If we do not compare our own children, then why do we compare His? Some of His children have various abilities and facets that sparkle in a unique way—they have pretty eyes. Let's not com-pare one rare treasure with another.

(See the *Personal Ministry Guide* at the end of this book to process the issue of worthlessness.)

CHAPTER ELEVEN

CRYING OVER SPILLED MILK

Shame

When the woman saw that the tree was good for food, and that it was a delight to the eyes, and that the tree was desirable to make one wise, she took from its fruit and ate; and she gave also to her husband with her, and he ate. Then the eyes of both of them were opened, and they knew that they were naked; and they sewed fig leaves together and made themselves loin coverings. They heard the sound of the Lord God walking in the garden in the cool of the day, and the man and his wife hid themselves from the presence of the Lord God among the trees of the garden (Genesis 3:6-8).

The Portrait of Shame

It was the end of the day and the sun had crossed the pinnacle of the sky. The man and woman had been occupied for several hours with their work in the garden and were returning to their place of rest. They could already feel the breeze growing cooler. It was fast approaching that time each day when the Creator-Friend came to talk with them.

As she walked through the garden, the woman glanced through the lush green vegetation to see the tree in the midst of Eden, whose fruit was weighed down with juicy sweetness, inviting her to quench her deep thirst and recover from the day's labor. It looked so good, and she could only imagine what it tasted like. But the word from the Creator was clear: "Don't eat from this tree, or you will surely die."

The woman, though, couldn't stop looking at the tree. "Something" told her that it had to be good for them. *Why would the Creator-Friend withhold the very best from us? How can something that looks so good be so bad? Surely He is mistaken, or maybe we didn't hear Him right.* It just could not be that they were to leave this tree and its luscious fruit alone.

The woman approached the tree cautiously, the thought of the taste of its fruit overwhelming the words and warning of the Creator-Friend. She reached out for the fruit with the man standing mute beside her. Pulling the fruit from the tree and taking it into her hand, she looked at it for a moment, and then, closing her eyes, bit into the fruit. Its juice filled her mouth and awakened her senses. It was delicious.

The woman handed the fruit to her husband, passing along the experience. He, in turn, bit into the fruit and wiped the excess juice from his lips. Anticipating some kind of thrill of delight, he was surprised to experience an immediate sick feeling of regret. The fruit, which seconds earlier had awakened their senses, now tasted like the clay they stood on. A brown deadness began to permeate their bodies, beginning with their mouths and radiating throughout to their extremities. It was as though the sun was setting prematurely and life was bleeding out of them with every beat of their hearts.

Finally, they came to an intense reality that they were alone. It was as though flesh had been amputated from the spirit. It was like a fingernail cut off and lying dead and useless—separate. The intimate connection between flesh and spirit—that realm where God spoke of His love for them—was now blank and void. They were filled with a new sensation—one they had not known, that no creature had known. It was a feeling of a vacuous and naked aloneness.

Man and woman were suddenly aware that they were disconnected from the Creator. They were puny and vulnerable. Shaken, they grabbed leaves off the trees and hurriedly wove them together to conceal their nakedness. Where their minds had been so able and ready to hear the thoughts of the Creator, now they could hear only the sound of their own accelerated heartbeats and thoughts of sheer terror.

And then came the sound of footsteps…

The Influence of Shame

The lie of shame is "*I am not good enough.*" It is a lie involving comparison, similar to worthlessness; but instead of comparing ourselves to other people, we compare ourselves to some kind of standard. Shame makes me want to cover myself in some way to hide my perceived imperfections.

There is a common phrase that some parents speak over their own child when he or she does something wrong or something that displeases them. The parents may say, "Shame on you." The unfortunate result of this pronouncement is that shame does come upon the child. Shame makes the child recoil and hang his head, not to mention that it cuts him off from relationship with the parent. Nothing good can happen when we say, "Shame on you." Nothing!

When our girls were small, occasionally they would spill some milk at the table. I think there is some kind of clause in the baby contract that a small child must spill something at the table at least once a day. In any case, it is inevitable that toddlers will spill the milk. As parents, we have basically one of two options as to how we respond. We can either yell something at them that they already know—namely, that they spilled their milk. Or we can grab a towel and clean up the mess.

Our response usually was (though not always, I'm sorry to say) to clean up the milk and then deal with the cause, if there was one. If we would have just gone off on them without doing anything about the mess, declaring that they were careless or stupid for spilling their drink, the milk would have lain on the table and begun to stink after a few days. The stink of that spilled milk is synonymous with the shame of past sin or shortfalls for which we believe there is no healing or forgiveness. When we are under the influence of shame, we are, in effect, "crying over spilled milk." We are focusing on the mess of the past without seeing the way to clean it up. Shame is the result of "stinkin' thinkin' " about God and His grace. Shame tends to remove us from the very place that God wants us to be—namely, with Him.

Shame is the Canaanite influence. The Hebrew name *Canaan* suggests humiliation. It was Canaan, the grandson of Noah, whose descendants bore the shame of the sin of looking upon Noah's drunken nakedness following the flood. Shame and nakedness go together throughout the Bible. When we are naked, we are exposed, vulnerable, and defenseless. Our reaction to shame or nakedness is to hide from one another, from God, and even from ourselves.

We need to be clear here that shame is the serpent's idea, not God's. We were created for intimate fellowship with God. Before the Fall, man looked forward to the distinct sound of God's footsteps in the cool of the day because they portended a wonderful fellowship with the Creator-Friend. But when we hear the sound of God's footsteps while living under the influence of shame, we reach for the nearest fig leaf.

Shame is, above all, the belief that we have crossed over a line that is beyond the grace of God. When we live under the influence of shame, we say to ourselves, "I have gone too far; there is no forgiveness for me." Of course, that is a lie. Lines do not limit the love of God.

The love of God is the most sovereign force in the universe. God loves out of His sovereignty without condition because He is God and does not need anything from us. What, after all, can we do for God? What can we give to Him that didn't come from Him in the first place? God declares, "If I were hungry I would not tell you, for the world is Mine, and all it contains" (Ps. 50:12). No line, no sin, can keep God from calling us back to Himself. God won't quit! God is not intimidated by lines I draw in the sand by my sin. Sin may control us sometimes, but it does not control God.

As with the other lies and influences we have discussed, shame results in its own list of effects and feelings.

Emotional Profile of Shame

He said, "I heard the sound of You in the garden, and I was afraid because I was naked; so I hid myself" (Genesis 3:10).

Genesis 3:10 gives us a kind of schematic of shame's effects. Shame begins with some kind of infraction or sin, which leaves us with a feeling of guilt, which leads to self-consciousness, which leads to fear, which leads to covering up and separation.

Guilt

The primary picture of guilt is that of a weight we carry. One of the New Testament words for guilt, *hupodikos*, implies that we are under or beneath judgment, as if it is weighing on us. David had the same descriptive feelings of his own guilt. "When I kept silent about my sin, my body wasted away through my groaning all day long. For day and night Your hand was heavy upon me; my vitality was drained away as with the fever heat of summer" (Ps. 32:3-4). David was being crushed beneath the burden of unconfessed sin. Shame is the crushing burden of our failure that we carry so unnecessarily.

Guilt in itself is not a bad thing until it crushes and immobilizes us into shame. While guilt is like a burden that can be handed over to the Lord for forgiveness, shame is more like defiling toxic mud—a crazy glue from hell that binds us to sin and prevents us from receiving the Lord's presence and the restoration of forgiveness.

Shame is therefore a blending of guilt and hopelessness that produces death in us. As Paul writes, "For the sorrow that is according to the will of God produces a repentance without regret, leading to salvation, but the sorrow of the world produces death" (2 Cor. 7:10). Guilt is a good and godly thing that can lead us back to God. It is the province of the Holy Spirit who convicts us of sin (see Jn. 16:8). Whereas, shame begins when we hide and see no way out of our sin. If we perceive God to be like an unforgiving and detached grandfather who is never pleased, shame will keep us in our guilt and separated from God.

It is important to recognize that we are not always guilty of the things that become sources of shame. We may *feel* guilty because we have not met someone else's expectation, but that does not mean we *are* guilty. Actually, perfectionism is a form of shame. We measure ourselves by a standard and come up wanting. Perfectionists believe that anything short of perfection is unacceptable—they learned that somewhere, usually at home.

I sat with a man one day who remembered bringing home a report card with something like all "A-'s" (A minuses). His parents (unlike mine, who would have been delighted and shocked at such a good report) said that if he would just work a little harder, he could get straight A's. He was, to say the least, never able to please his parents.

We have many expectations handed down to us that are not of God. But no matter what they are or where they came from, God does not require us to haul our sins around our necks as penance. That is a religious concept, but it is not a God thing.

A number of years ago there was a movie titled *The Mission* in which a conquistador killed another man in a sword fight. The man went to the priest and was told to do penance for the death by chaining his armor to himself, representing the guilt of his sin. In this way, he would bear the weight of what he had done.

There came a time when the man became exhausted with the weight of his armor/sin. As he was climbing a hill and could no longer bear the weight of the armor/sin, he began to fall backward. Just as he was at the end of his strength, someone cut the armor loose, allowing the armor/sin to fall away and free the man. That weight he carried represented guilt, and the chain that bound him to it was shame.

Self-consciousness and Hiding

Along with a burden of guilt comes the knowledge of our sheer nakedness—our powerlessness over sin.

Shame focuses us on whatever is naked and vulnerable. Shame leads us to cover up our weakness or vulnerability. David said that his sin was always before him (see Ps. 51:3). In other words, he was preoccupied with it; it ruled his life. Shame allows us little opportunity to see God because we are so focused on our nakedness. It is a feeling of humiliation and exposure.

When we live under shame, we tend to cover up as Adam did by sewing some fig leaves together. Those fig leaves are whatever we can muster to conceal our exposure. They may be our own legalistic system or some kind of works we do in order to feel worthy again. Those works, like fig leaves, are worthless as a covering. They tend to unravel over time, leaving us naked again. The only alternative is to go to God—to respond to His invitation of restoration—and allow Him to clothe us with Christ.

Those who live under shame tend to hide themselves, perhaps by becoming the class clown, by making fun of themselves, or even by total denial. We also may cover ourselves by deflecting blame to someone else as Adam did when he said that it was the woman who tempted him.

Whatever the method, we spend our time focused on whatever is exposed. Shame is like a bad check that hasn't cleared your account. You dread its arrival at the bank and do everything you can to cover it before it does. Shame is the chronic feeling of insufficient means to cover a shortfall.

Bob was a brilliant man who taught high school math and economics. In our initial interview with Bob, it was very clear that he spent a lot of time trying to compensate and cover up for his imperfections. He was a very cerebral man who felt that he or anyone else could never do anything well enough. Though he had a strong faith, he was not sure how God really felt about him personally. Bob lived under the influence of shame.

During our ministry time, the Lord brought Bob to the memory of when he was very young and his family had visited friends in the East. Before the end of their visit, Bob made some kind of silly remark to the family friends about their visit with them, which the friends laughed off as a feeble attempt at nine-year-old humor. His parents had a different opinion, however.

No sooner had they pulled out of the driveway than Bob's parents began to yell at him in the most demeaning way. They told him that he had embarrassed them in front of the family and said, "Shame on you!" Bob was crushed and melted into the floor of the backseat with his parents ending their tirade and giving him the silent treatment for the rest of the trip.

Fear and Separation

We already have spent an entire chapter on fear, but it is important to know, again, that the origin of fear is our separation from God. Adam said that he and Eve heard the sound of God's footsteps in the garden and became afraid. The source of the fear was their independence from God and the uncertainty of what might now happen to them.

When Adam and Eve chose to doubt God, they became separated from Him. They who were spiritual beings in close communion with God turned into two naked people in the midst of the garden. Shame and nakedness were felt for the first time ever. Only a little while before, when they were in communion with God, were they naked and not ashamed (see Gen. 2:25). But when they were separated from God and alone in their own frailty, shame set in. Shame is the focus on our sin and powerlessness to the exclusion of God's grace.

When the man and his wife heard the sound of God's footsteps, they ran away from Him instead of toward Him. We are so worried about the expectation of punishment that we miss the invitation of God to repent and be restored. Where God's intention for us is to be hidden in Him (see Col. 3:3), shame makes us hide *from* Him.

Where we read about David falling into adultery with Bathsheba and subsequently murdering her husband, we have no information about his living close to the Lord. There are no psalms of praise and intimacy with God. He was separated by his sin and living in denial. One wonders how David conducted the affairs of state or his role as king/worshiper. Shame reduced David to living and ruling in his own strength (as it always does), because he was separated from the presence of God. It is important to know that this was not God's idea. God eventually sent the prophet Nathan to lance the boil of David's sin that lived beneath the surface of his life.

Shame tells us that when we cross the line with God, His grace is not sufficient for us. But fortunately, David begged God for grace when his sin was uncovered. He said, "Be gracious to me, O God, according to Your lovingkindness" (Ps. 51:1a). When we live under shame, grace eludes us. We are fixed on our sin and not the Lord. Shame causes the weight of our sin to crush the life of God out of us. We hang our heads and can no longer look up to see God.

Covering Up

For those old enough to recall the days of Richard Nixon and the Watergate scandal, we remember one phrase that caused great trouble for our late president and some of his associates. They were not guilty of the break-in itself, but the *cover-up* that had followed. Attempting to hide the fact that something illegal and unethical had taken place was as bad as the actual crime, because it attempted to sweep sin under the rug. And the problem with sweeping things under the rug is that it tends to make lumpy carpets. The dirt is still there and will never actually be dealt with as long as it is hidden.

Covering up is one of our carnal responses to sin. We may not have fig leaves readily available to us, but we still reach for some kind of disguise or covering. The cover-up may consist of doing some kind of works to try to hide our nakedness. Some of us get involved in ministry out of guilt rather than compassion, believing that we can somehow compensate for our failure by doing good. Or, some of us become perfectionists, hoping to cover our own inadequacies by holding everyone to an unattainable standard. The end result of inadequate works or self-perfection is that we never seem to be able to do enough or be good enough.

Those who live under the influence of shame act as though God uses some kind of cosmic scales upon which He weighs the good things against the bad things. But God is not an accountant and He has no scales. If He did, we could never hope to do enough good to outweigh our shortfalls. Instead, our approach to God should be one of radical acceptance of His grace. The blood of Christ has tipped the scales in our favor. What can we add to that?

The problem with fig leaves is that they do not cover much and they always come apart. Whatever we do rather than face God with our sin and failure, whatever we do instead of throwing ourselves on His all-sufficient grace, will not get it done. The dirt will still be under the carpet. We will trip over it again.

Shame, fear, and separation are not God's ideas. There is much more to His love than we can hope to understand. The truth is that God is bent on cleaning up the mess—calling us back to intimacy with Him.

The Truth About Shame

When I was about six years old, our family lived on the Chestnut Ridge in western Pennsylvania. Somewhere along the line my mom received a new hurricane lamp with two floral globes trimmed in gold. She placed it on a table in a prominent place so as to give light over the whole room, and she was, as I recall, very pleased with this new lamp.

One day, as little boys will do, especially twin boys, my brother and I were playing in the living room, throwing a ball back and forth. On one of the "forths," I threw the ball a little too hard and wide of my brother. Although *he* missed the ball, the lamp caught it. With that, the top globe of the lamp fell off and broke on the floor. I was in shock.

This was Mom's new, prized lamp, and I had broken it. Quickly, I took the damaged part of the lamp and hid it in the closet so that it would not be found. Then I packed whatever I could think of in a pillowcase and set off to forge a new life in the woods across the road. I knew that I had gone too far this time, and I would face death if I stayed around. So I went about 50 feet into the woods and watched for my parents to come home. (Our grandmother was watching us while they were away.)

After what seemed like days, but was in fact probably minutes, my grandmother called to me, telling me to come into the house. How did she know where I was? She must have been watching the entire time. She called, "It's time to come home, Tommy. Come back into the house." Of course, I could not ignore my grandmother, so I journeyed the 50 feet and returned home.

She then wasted no time asking me about the missing globe, and I had to tell her what had happened and where I had hidden it. She said something like, "You know better than to play like that in the house. It will be okay; we will get another globe." My sentence had been commuted, and I was no longer the dead twin walking.

Shame had made me afraid and sent me into the woods. I'm sure I still go running into the woods sometimes, but the sound of "It's time to come home" will call me back, if I listen.

God Already Knows What We Are Trying to Hide

And there is no creature hidden from His sight, but all things are open and laid bare to the eyes of Him with whom we have to do (Hebrews 4:13).

The truth is that God was there to see the milk get knocked over. He was there and is still there waiting to bring you the truth about His love and grace in your life. Therefore, stop crying over spilled milk and let the Lord remove the shame that prevents you from fellowshipping with Him.

When I think of the grace of God, I go to that scene in the garden. Because there are no God-free zones in the universe, we know that God heard the sound of that fruit core hit the ground. God knew exactly what had happened, and yet He came looking for the man and woman anyway. I see and imagine the Lord Himself coming with a bucket and a mop, so to speak, to clean up the mess. God was sitting at the table when the milk was spilled! He saw the whole thing, yet His response was to come calling, "Adam, where are you?"

The reality of God's grace and heart toward cleaning up the mess was made clear when Jesus taught His disciples about servanthood. When they were in the upper room, Jesus grabbed a towel and a basin and showed them how to be like Himself. They were supposed to wash one another's feet and clean off the residual sin and the world from one another. The message is clear: No one should be kept from the table of God's grace.

God Calls Us to Himself

Then the Lord God called to the man, and said to him, "Where are you?" (Genesis 3:9)

"Where are you?" The question still resounds in our spiritual ears each time we fall into sin. God is not satisfied to leave us in the bushes. He calls to us and invites us to repentance and restoration in His presence. When man was created, he was naked and not ashamed because he was in relationship with God and dependent upon Him body, soul, and spirit. Then when we sin, when we blow it, God's response is to call us back into intimate fellowship. He calls out to us, "Where are you?"

Our problem is that we have a human and finite idea of the love of God. We are flawed and needy humans who seldom love without reason. We usually have a reason or rationale upon which to pin our affections for others—even our love of God. We love God more because of what He has done than for who He is.

John, "that disciple whom Jesus loved" (Jn. 21:7), tells us that we hide from God because we just don't understand the extravagant love of God.

> *We have come to know and have believed the love which God has for us. God is love, and the one who abides in love abides in God, and God abides in him. By this, love is perfected with us, so that we may have confidence in the day of judgment; because as He is, so also are we in this world. There is no fear in love; but perfect love casts out fear, because fear involves punishment, and the one who fears is not perfected in love. We love, because He first loved us* (1 John 4:16-19).

We can trust the love of God. His love is *perfect* love—a mature love, which means that it does not need anything else to be love. It is unconditional. God does not need us to do anything to enable Him to love us. He is not a man who needs His ego stroked or for us to give Him reason to love us.

God's love stems from His nature. "God is love" (1 Jn. 4:8b). Your sin may control you sometimes, but it does not control God. God wants you to trust Him and stop trying to live in your own power for your own pleasure and glory. Paul says "if you confess with your mouth Jesus as Lord, and believe in your heart that God raised Him from the dead, you will be saved; for with the heart a person believes, resulting in righteousness, and with the mouth he confesses, resulting in salvation" (Rom. 10:9-10).

God Is Not Separated From Us by Our Nakedness

Who will separate us from the love of Christ? Will tribulation, or distress, or persecution, or famine, or nakedness, or peril, or sword? (Romans 8:35)

God knows us in our nakedness; He used to change our diapers. Make no mistake, God does not accept our sin—just as we would not approve of the sin and rebellion of our own kids. But God sees us as we see our children—as His own precious possessions. I don't look at, nor do I remember, the countless cups of milk my children have spilled. I see only my babies. So does God.

The truth is that none of us is perfect, none of us faithful. But God is perfect even when we are not perfect. Paul told Timothy that "if we are faithless, He remains faithful, for He cannot deny Himself" (2 Tim. 2:13). God cannot deny His own nature, which is one of sovereign love. He cannot help but to love us and invite us back into fellowship by the blood of Jesus Christ, dirty diapers and all.

Christ Took Our Nakedness to the Cross

Fixing our eyes on Jesus, the author and perfecter of faith, who for the joy set before Him endured the cross, despising the shame, and has sat down at the right hand of the throne of God (Hebrews 12:2).

Jesus was naked and not ashamed because of His relationship with the Father. He took our nakedness upon Himself so that we could be clothed with His own righteousness. "For all of you who were baptized into Christ have clothed yourselves with Christ" (Gal. 3:27). No more fig leaves! God meets us in our guilt with grace, as the psalm says: "You enlarge my steps under me, and my feet have not slipped" (Ps. 18:36). God has cleaned up the spill so that it will not stink up our relationship with Him. More than anything else, God wants us to be with Him. *No more crying over spilled milk!*

(See the *Personal Ministry Guide* at the end of this book to process the issue of shame.)

CHAPTER TWELVE

LIVING ON THE LEDGE

Insecurity

The king said, "Is there not yet anyone of the house of Saul to whom I may show the kindness of God?" And Ziba said to the king, "There is still a son of Jonathan who is crippled in both feet." So the king said to him, "Where is he?" And Ziba said to the king, "Behold, he is in the house of Machir the son of Ammiel in Lo-debar." Then King David sent and brought him from the house of Machir the son of Ammiel, from Lo-debar (2 Samuel 9:3-5).

The Portrait of Insecurity

Mephibosheth was a handsome young man, born a prince over his people, the grandson of Saul, king of Israel. At one time he had anticipated life when people would bow at his approach, interrupting their lives just to catch a glimpse of this anointed son.

But the course of events drastically changed his future and Mephibosheth became the last in line of the house of Saul. Both his grandfather and his father, Jonathan, had been killed in battle years before when he was a five-year-old boy. After hearing the shocking news of their deaths, Mephibosheth's nurse picked him up to flee, and as she hurried to leave, he fell. The fall left him crippled, powerless for life. Then his own brother was murdered by those who were trying to gain the favor of the new king.

Now the heir to the throne of Israel was hiding out on the backside of nowhere in Lo-debar, far from the security of the walls of Jerusalem. He lived in the guest house of a wealthy man, which was perched on a small ridge. From there he could see the approach of any threat.

It was the custom in those days for a new king to wipe out any remaining family members of the previous king who might pose a threat. Mephibosheth lived under the worry of a continuous threat from every corner. He could trust no one and felt safe with no one. This should-have-been prince now lived under constant fear of even the servants of the king who now reigned over God's people. He and his family learned to sleep with one eye open—to live with a readiness to run at the slightest hint of danger. There was no rest, no place of repose where they could simply enjoy life.

Day by day Mephibosheth sat by the window watching for a dust cloud that might betray the arrival of an informant. Then finally, the time had come when perched on the ledge of his mountain sanctuary, he could see the dust of an approaching rider.

The Influence of Insecurity

The lie that inspires insecurity is "*I am not safe.*" Mephibosheth lived under the influence of what is best described as *insecurity*. He did not feel safe. Insecurity is the influence of the Perizzites, which comes from the Hebrew word *paratz*. It conveys the sense of being out in the open and unprotected. The simple meaning of the word is the best interpretation, and that is "someone who believes he lives in a place of vulnerability."

To be insecure is to live with a feeling of being unprotected, unsafe, powerless, or distracted. The insecure spend their time crunched up in a ball of self-protection and seldom get close to or trust anyone. They live on the ledge, watching for the next attack. Everything is a threat.

People who live under the influence of insecurity try to take control in any way possible. Controlling efforts may range from building walls of self-protection to becoming the one who is always taking responsibility. We may seem mature, adult-like, and responsible, but in fact, our overly responsible behavior is a way to merely feel in control.

Emotional Profile of Insecurity

Andrew was a bright young man in his late 20's who, to all appearances, had everything going for him. He was insightful and sensitive, but he also was one who lived with one eye open, so to speak. He was jittery and sometimes volatile in his marriage and even in his work. Though he was very articulate, he found it hard to read or to stay focused on any task.

This bright and articulate young man and his wife came for ministry to get to the root of some of his fear and anxiety. During our initial time together and in the subsequent prayer time, several memories arose of a childhood that was, at best, unpredictable. Andrew had grown up in a secluded compound in the rural South amidst the poverty of a single-parent household. He and his brothers were raised by his mother, who kept them away from others.

The children of this family, and especially Andrew, also lived under constant threat of severe and abusive punishment from their mother. The slightest thing of daily life would set her off into a rage that frequently included violence against her children. The mother would sometimes beat the children, chiefly Andrew, for no apparent reason other than her own anger and feelings of frustration. In fact, Andrew was regularly awakened during the night by his mother beating him with a broomstick or whatever else was handy. Needless to say, Andrew was never able to be at rest, and consequently, he slept every night with one eye open.

One particular memory that held much pain was one in which Andrew's mother sent him to find something in the pantry. Andrew looked for several minutes and could not find what his mother asked him for. Feelings of terror began to sweep over Andrew as he remembered the episode in vivid detail. He had the feeling that someone was about to beat him, to harm him in some way. (It reminded him of a similar feeling that he was experiencing at his current job, where he was filling orders in a warehouse.) Andrew felt alone and very vulnerable as the scene of terror filled his mind. He believed that he was then, and was now, totally unprotected and had no control. He was living under the influence of insecurity.

When we asked the Lord to reveal His perspective on Andrew's remembered horror, the Lord spoke no words, but instead revealed Himself to Andrew as a surrounding presence. At first, Andrew was only vaguely aware of a presence around him in that pantry. But as the revelation unfolded, Andrew was aware of it in a more physical way in the form of a human hug. The truth was that Andrew was not alone and that the situation was in the hands of a loving and ever-present Father.

It is important to note that history did not change and that the abuse continued. But the wound no longer controlled Andrew, nor did the lie that no one was in control of the situation.

Andrew was a sort of modern-day Mephibosheth. He constantly felt unsafe, living on the ledge. Those who live on the ledge of insecurity usually experience feelings of anxiety, vulnerability, distrustfulness, and that everything is out of control. By definition, the strongest aspect of insecurity is the issue of control—or the lack of it.

Fear, Anxiety

Perhaps the most obvious effect of insecurity is fear or anxiety. Those who live under the influence of insecurity find themselves crunched up in a corner somewhere waiting for the next wave of attacks to hit their defenses.

We spoke in Chapter Eight that the greatest fear is that of being alone, and there is a terrifying, empty aloneness that accompanies insecurity as well. Imagine Mephibosheth living on the side of a mountain, in terror that he might be discovered at any moment, that his life was no more secure than he alone could make it. When we live under insecurity, we believe that our life is in our own hands and we are terrified.

Threatened, Lack of Control

The Scriptures compare the insecure to a city whose walls are broken down. "Like a city that is broken into and without walls is a man who has no control over his spirit" (Prov. 25:28). It may be that we were raised in some kind of unsafe environment over which we had no control. We may have had an alcoholic or abusive parent like Andrew's mother or perhaps no parents at all, instead growing up on the streets. Some who live under insecurity may have been molested in some way and feel threatened when anyone invades their personal space. Whatever the source or reason, these people live outside the walls of protection.

The insecure believe that they are living life alone and that no one is watching out for them. They feel the need to control absolutely everything—from the way others see them to where they sit in a restaurant. They have to be in control of their environment and feel threatened when they are not. They are like Mephibosheth living on top of a ridge so that he could see any approaching threat.

People who live in insecurity also feel the need to control others. They do so by manipulating people's emotions, as in using anger to make them afraid or pity to make them ashamed. They also may try to control others by sarcastic wit, which makes people reluctant to approach them. By whatever means, the insecure must be in control or they are out of control.

Those who feel threatened by insecurity—the ones whose walls have been torn down—will inevitably try to build other walls in order to feel safe and in control. These are walls of comfort. They will try to find comfort in things like food, sex, drugs, alcohol, new clothes, new cars or houses, or anything else over which they can exercise some kind of control. They build walls of addiction, manipulation, dissociation, indifference, or even compulsive behaviors. There are many strategies by which the unsafe build walls.

Books could be and have been written on each of the various results of feeling out of control. But the underlying reason for these behaviors is that people just don't feel safe. They are threatened by everything and everyone.

Volatile, Impulsive

There is a good reason for the little no-smoking sign that appears on gasoline pumps. The slightest spark from a cigarette could touch off a major explosion. The gas and particularly its fumes are very unstable or volatile. Those who live with insecure people know something about volatility. They know that the slightest spark can set off the most unreasonable responses.

Things that seem to be of little importance threaten the security of those who live on the ledge. As Proverbs 25:28 says, the insecure person has "no control over his spirit."

When it seems that our walls have been torn down leaving us unprotected, we feel threatened by the slightest provocation and will put up a wall of anger that tells those around us, "Don't mess with me!" This keeps people out of range so they cannot threaten our safety zone.

This volatility is a different type of anger than what grows out of rejection. Rejection leads to a constant, seething kind of anger. The kind of anger that comes with insecurity, on the other hand, is a circumstantial, unpredictable, and intense kind of anger. It is what some might call a "short fuse."

We have seen this kind of anger in teens who feel unsafe because they have no boundaries. Children, especially teens, need some kind of boundaries to help them feel safe. When we remove structure, we also remove their security. The results are explosive.

People who have suffered abuse of all kinds frequently feel trapped or frustrated by circumstances that remind them of the abuse they suffered. For instance, we have seen both men and women who were sexually abused who cannot tolerate anyone coming into their space. They feel trapped, encroached upon, and they respond to this trapped feeling like a frightened, cornered animal. They fight. When someone explodes in our faces, he or she is probably doing so because we are too close. We need to learn to respect personal perimeters and back off.

Volatile anger stems mostly from some feeling of frustration. It's like we are pushing against something heavy that refuses to budge no matter how hard we push. We get red in the face as we push and strain with all our might, but nothing moves. This is the look on the face of a baby who loses control of his bottle. It's that scrunched-up look that erupts into a red-faced tantrum. The problem is not that the baby is spoiled; the problem is that what he needs is out of his control.

Another response to insecurity is impulsiveness. Those who are insecure tend to live their lives according to whatever circumstances arise. For example, they may buy things out of fear of missing a good deal or fear of looking foolish, rather than take the time to think about what makes sense for them. They are impulsive; they are compelled to react to the world rather than respond in what others think are rational, sensible ways. In the end, people who act impulsively are not merely unwise; they are also unsafe.

When we are faced with what seems to be irrational anger, we need to get hold of our own security and then look beyond the explosion to where we will find a threatened child.

Defensive, Distrustful

The people on the ledge live there because it is defendable. People who live under the influence of insecurity feel that they must protect themselves from any threat, even verbal threats. They can never lose a point or give in to an argument, for to do so shatters their security. They must be right at all costs! They are perched on the edge of self-survival.

For them, a discussion is not a discussion; it's an assault on the fortress of self. Remember the story about two men who "discussed" what kind of cars they had? The angry man's reaction was not about a car; it was about his feeling threatened by the slightest whiff of disagreement. The man who bought the new car felt that his integrity was being attacked and had to defend himself. It seems irrational unless you are familiar with living on the ledge. There it makes perfect sense.

Another defense is simply not to trust anyone at all. Those who feel insecure find it very hard to form new relationships because relationships require trust. They cannot trust anyone. To trust is to let someone in, and that is just too much to risk. People must be kept out at all costs.

Powerless, Helpless

Mephibosheth was lame in both feet. In other words, he was completely powerless, helpless, and immobilized in his disability. This is how the insecure see themselves: powerless, lame, helpless.

Many times they feel powerless in the origin of their insecurity. They may have been abused or terrorized at a young age, at a time when they could do nothing to protect themselves. Whenever their feelings of insecurity are triggered, they return to that same young age. My wife and I have found ourselves ministering to many children in grown-up bodies. Something became disconnected at the time of abuse and stopped growing.

Often I have found that those who live the loudest are the ones who feel the lamest. In other words, they compensate for their powerless immobility by directing everyone around them. They are the bullies who push kids around on the schoolyard but are themselves being beaten and terrorized at home. The only way they can achieve any kind of power is to terrorize someone else. The boss who yells at his employees is repeating the sound that still rings in his own ears. He is yelling out of his own powerlessness. He is less a bully than a beaten child trying to feel safe.

Me Against the World

Those who live on the ledge are usually there by themselves. The reason is obvious: Who can they trust to be there with them? It's not that they don't want anyone else there. It's that they can't risk having anyone else there. Mephibosheth had no choice but to live a solitary life in order to avoid the threat of discovery by the king and possible death.

Those who live on the ledge live for themselves and by themselves. They feel like it's them against the world. Their lives spin in a centripetal pattern in which everything leads back to self.

Those on the ledge are constantly on the lookout for approaching threats. Although there are many indications of insecurity, ranging from denial to xenophobia, they all stem from the same belief that says, "I am not safe."

The Truth About Insecurity

Mephibosheth, the son of Jonathan the son of Saul, came to David and fell on his face and prostrated himself. And David said, "Mephibosheth." And he said,

"Here is your servant!" David said to him, "Do not fear, for I will surely show kindness to you for the sake of your father Jonathan, and will restore to you all the land of your grandfather Saul; and you shall eat at my table regularly." Again he prostrated himself and said, "What is your servant, that you should regard a dead dog like me?" Then the king called Saul's servant Ziba and said to him, "All that belonged to Saul and to all his house I have given to your master's grandson. You and your sons and your servants shall cultivate the land for him, and you shall bring in the produce so that your master's grandson may have food; nevertheless Mephibosheth your master's grandson shall eat at my table regularly." Now Ziba had fifteen sons and twenty servants. Then Ziba said to the king, "According to all that my lord the king commands his servant so your servant will do." So Mephibosheth ate at David's table as one of the king's sons. Mephibosheth had a young son whose name was Mica. And all who lived in the house of Ziba were servants to Mephibosheth. So Mephibosheth lived in Jerusalem, for he ate at the king's table regularly. Now he was lame in both feet (2 Samuel 9:6-13).

The truth is that the King knows where we are, and He woos us off the ledge to His table. David, as a type of Christ, was not the typical usurper to the throne of Israel. He was placed there by God in the ultimate position of authority. Through a series of many battles, God gave him rest from his enemies (see 2 Sam. 7:1). So it was from this place of ultimate authority and total rest that David called and searched for someone to whom he could show kindness.

The Hebrew word for kindness here is *hesed*, which is the predisposition of God to demonstrate love for us. It is a bending, a stooping over to show us mercy. It is as though God's mercy is dripping over the railings of Heaven and falling on us. It is not something to which we are entitled; it is the unrestrained love of

God that searches us out to bring us to Himself. Grace flows from the source of total authority.

There is a great picture of grace in the Book of Esther. When Esther entered into the king's chambers without his permission, he had the authority to kill her on the spot; instead, he extended his scepter to her. She touched the top of it and remained alive because the king gave her grace (see Esther 5:2). The king gave her what she could not get for herself. She was powerless before his throne.

Grace flows from authority. Esther approached the king because she knew his heart. We can approach the King of Heaven the same way. He has called us to Himself, not to clobber us, but to love us. Grace, or kindness, is something we extend to someone who cannot obtain it for himself. We do it because we see that person's helplessness. It's like helping a turtle that is stuck on its back that would struggle and die without our intervention. When it comes to these inner healing issues, though, only God has the ability to turn our lives over again and set us right-side up on our feet.

There Is No Fear in God

We said before that "perfect love casts out fear" (1 Jn. 4:18). The first issue that the king dealt with was Mephibosheth's fear. David said, "Do not fear." We find our ultimate security in the One who is ultimately secure: God Himself. We can "set [our] mind on the things above, not on the things that are on earth [such as threats and things that make us insecure]. For [we] have died and [our] life is hidden with Christ in God" (Col. 3:2-3). We can look at God and know that He handles the threats. Nothing happens without God's knowing about it. God is our refuge and our stronghold. He is our hiding place. We are safe in His grace that flows from His total security.

The Lord is my light and my salvation; whom shall I fear? The Lord is the defense of my life; whom shall I dread? When evildoers came upon me to devour my flesh, my adversaries and my enemies, they stumbled and fell. Though a host encamp against me, my heart will not fear; though war arise against me, in spite of this I shall be confident. One thing I have asked from the Lord, that I shall seek: that I may dwell in the house of the Lord all the days of my life, to behold the beauty of the Lord and to meditate in His temple. For in the day of trouble He will conceal me in His tabernacle (Psalm 27:1-5a).

To be secure literally means to be without care. God is without care or concern. God is without fear. God is without rival. God is without want. And when we are in God, we are these things as well. Even when the world around us seems threatening—indeed, when bad things happen—we are still safe in God and confident in His love for us.

We Live at God's Table

David said that Mephibosheth would eat at his table as his own son. In the same way, the King of the universe puts His own mantle of sonship upon us and we are secure in Him alone. Our ultimate security is in the love and grace of God Himself. The King will not leave us on the ledge; rather, He brings us to His table.

Think for a minute about how Mephibosheth must have felt. Here was a man who was powerless and afraid, believing that he might be betrayed and discovered at any moment. He lived for years under the lie that he was in terrible danger and that his life was totally out of control. Now comes the messenger of the king, along with servants, to help Mephibosheth to a royal carriage. The king sent his own limousine to fetch this man to receive his grace.

Now Mephibosheth is before King David and throws himself at his feet, not knowing whether or not he will ever get up again. To his great astonishment, the king says, "Get up, and don't be afraid. I'm giving you everything your grandfather and father had and all the servants you need to carry you to the table. You're going to have breakfast, lunch, and dinner with me every day like one of my own sons."

Then, in what was the most telling moment, Mephibosheth was brought to the table at the hand of the king. He took his position there, his legs placed gently under the table. He was no longer lame, powerless, and defenseless. He was in the embrace of the king, his father's best friend.

The security we lost at someone's neglectful, disinterested, or abusive hand is now restored by the encompassing embrace of God as Father. We live securely within God's embrace—an embrace from which no one can remove us. Our lameness and insecurity are now under the King's table. The King relates to us solely on the basis of His own grace and provision. We are eternally secure at the table.

Now that we are secure in God, we can extend that grace to others. The very ones who abused us can be brought to the table themselves. Why? Jesus told us to pray for those who abuse us (see Lk. 6:28). In so doing, we extend to them the same grace that brought us to the table. When another person is hungry—when they need what is at the table—they can sit next to us. The grace that we extend to them is the grace of the King, and we are free to give that grace because we live safely in His embrace.

The Lord Surrounds Us

Philip was a young man in his early 30's who grew up in the inner city. He and his wife were struggling because of an extra-marital affair he had had. They found their way to our ministry center and began to pour out the pain of the experience. This seemed to be the end for them.

During the initial interview, it was revealed that Philip had been raised on the streets of the inner city. There was very little structure in his early life, and he had no father at home. Consequently, Philip struggled to feel settled and safe in his life. It was difficult for him to relate to his wife in any spiritually intimate way. He couldn't get close to his wife or anyone else. He never felt safe with anyone.

When we prayed for the Lord to show him the source of his insecurity, he was reminded of when he was very young, sitting all alone in the living room of the apartment where his family lived. He felt alone abandoned...unprotected...insecure. He believed that he could not trust anyone and that he would have to be the one to control his world. When we prayed for the Lord to show him the truth, the Lord seemed to surround him as if to embrace him.

Philip wept as, for perhaps the first time in his life, he felt safe and surrounded by love. Within minutes he was able to express his heartfelt, not legalistic, sorrow to his wife for the affair that had almost ended their marriage. He had looked for comfort and intimacy outside of his marriage. In that moment of truth, Philip was able to deal with his sin, and his wife was able to extend grace from a new perspective. She was given the opportunity to see inside Philip's heart and became aware of the circumstances that led to compromise. Healing began for both of them in the surrounding embrace of God's love.

The Scriptures are filled with promises of God's embracing presence for those who are secure in Him.

> *For it is You who blesses the righteous man, O Lord, You surround him with favor as with a shield* (Psalm 5:12).

> *Those who trust in the Lord are as Mount Zion, which cannot be moved but abides forever. As the mountains surround Jerusalem, so the Lord surrounds His people from this time forth and forever* (Psalm 125:1-2).

> *"Run, speak to that young man, saying, 'Jerusalem will be inhabited without walls because of the multitude of men and cattle within it. For I,' declares the Lord, 'will be a wall of fire around her, and I will be the glory in her midst' "* (Zechariah 2:4-5).

> *O Lord, how my adversaries have increased! Many are rising up against me. Many are saying of my soul, "There is no deliverance for him in God." Selah. But You, O Lord, are a shield about me, my glory, and the One who lifts my head* (Psalm 3:1-3).

Many are the sorrows of the wicked, but he who trusts in the Lord, lovingkindness shall surround him (Psalm 32:10).

The angel of the Lord encamps around those who fear Him, and rescues them (Psalm 34:7).

(See the *Personal Ministry Guide* at the end of this book to process the issue of insecurity.)

CHAPTER THIRTEEN

TORN SLEEVES

Defilement

The Portrait of Defilement

Tamar was a gentle rose coming to full bloom in the house of her father, the king. While she was growing into a virtuous and beautiful young woman, she lived in the safety of the compartment allotted to her mother's children within the trusting enclave of her family. Tamar was, in a word, innocent.

As all the virtuous daughters of the king, Tamar wore a white garment with long sleeves to declare her purity and her relationship to her father the king. All who saw her knew that she was as clean and pure as her flowing white sleeves. The garment she wore was an outward indication of her inward condition and her unique and untouched value to her family and her father. She was whole and untouched, a precious treasure.

One day, word came from the king that she was to go to the house of Amnon, her half-brother, to prepare some bread to strengthen him in his illness. His illness appeared to be serious enough to cause the issue of a royal command to Tamar. Being an obedient daughter, she gathered makings for some bread to strengthen her brother's heart and left immediately.

As she arrived at the house, the other servants were ministering to the firstborn son of David and doing what they could to make him comfortable. Amnon was the heir to David's throne and therefore the object of much attention and indulgence—indeed, overindulgence.

As Tamar prepared bread for her brother, she took some in her hand and gave it to him, but he refused to eat it. After ordering everyone to leave the room, Amnon, pretending to be weak, said, "Please bring the bread into the bedroom." Of course, Tamar saw nothing wrong with going into the bedroom of her own half-brother. He was family—he was sickly—he was safe.

As Tamar stretched out her hand to give her brother the bread she had made, he slapped the bread to the side and grabbed her. Seized by a numbing horror of what was about to happen, she gasped, "Stop!" But Amnon could not be persuaded. Tamar pleaded, "This is wrong…you are my half-brother. How can you do this? This is against the law of God. Please…stop!"

Now Amnon, who only moments before seemed too weak to eat, grabbed Tamar with the force of demonic lust. He threw her down and overpowered her innocent frailty, raping his own half-sister.

After only moments of sexual gratification and molestation, Amnon's lust turned to disgust, and he pushed her away in anger. He had taken all that was precious from her and left her white sleeves as a mocking reminder of her lost wholeness.

"Throw this girl out of here!" Amnon shouted to his servant. "She is of no further use to me."

"No, Amnon. Please don't do this. Everyone will think this was my fault. They saw me going into your bedroom. I will be ruined. Please don't—please don't."

But Amnon turned away from her, and his servant dragged Tamar out of the room, slamming the door behind her. She was left out in the dark—discarded like a dead animal along the road.

Now the white sleeves that denoted her purity only minutes earlier seemed to mock her broken and used condition. She tore them from her garment in mournful resignation. Picking up the dust from the ground, she threw it on her head, declaring her lostness. In those fleeting seconds, her life, with all its expectation and hope, was rubbed out, compromised. She was inconsolable in her grief.

When the king heard of all that happened he became angry, but he did nothing, which added fuel to Tamar's sense of loss. Her grief was public, but the sin against her was private. No one would ever know. No one would ever believe her.

Tamar stayed in the house of her brother Absalom, desolate and ruined. (See Second Samuel 13:6-20.)

The Influence of Defilement

The lie that inspires the influence of defilement is *"I am ruined for life."* To defile something is to make it unclean. It is like taking a vessel filled with pure water and introducing one drop of sewage. Even though the filth may not be visible to the naked eye, it renders the water unfit for human consumption. It is unclean, defiled. Whatever is defiled is dirty, bad, unfit.

Defilement is the *Hivite* influence. The word *Hivite* comes from the Hebrew word *havah*, which suggests natural or carnal life. It is the root from which Eve's name is taken. For the purpose of this book, we will say that the Hivites refer to a base or natural impulse—the natural life as opposed to the spiritual.

The references we find to the Hivites always seem to be associated with some kind of deception or perverse abuse. It was Shechem, the son of Hamor the Hivite, who lured Dinah to a place where he could rape and defile her (see Gen. 34:2). And it was the men of Gibeon, ethnically Hivites, who tricked the camp of Israel into making a covenant with them to avoid certain death (see Josh. 9:3-15). When we see the influence of the Hivites, we see defilement and deception.

The influence of defilement has several key components: abuse, an innocent or helpless victim, an overpowering abuser, and disregard for the victim. All of these leave the victim—the defiled—with a sense that he or she is ruined for life. Many times, in fact most of the time in our experience, the abuser is close to the victim and should have been trustworthy, so there is also a strong sense of betrayal.

Defilement does not happen exclusively because of sexual assault of some kind. The ruin of defilement comes as the result of betrayed innocence.

My father was a good and decent man who worked for the same company for 35 years. He was a dedicated employee, a company man. He gave his best year after year and eventually became the head of his department. He was there to guard the office when the labor union went on strike. He worked Saturdays on special projects when the load was heavy. He picked up his family and moved hundreds of miles away when the company needed him to. He was a true company man. When he reached the age of 55, he could see that he was headed for the homestretch toward retirement. Given his long and faithful service to the company, he expected to work another 15 years or so and then retire on the full pension he had worked so long to accrue. But it didn't quite work out that way.

One day as he was working at his desk, two men walked into his office wearing polite but impersonal smiles. Out of the blue they informed him that he and the senior people in his department would be phased out, necessitating an early retirement, that the company was moving in another direction with younger men. With a pat on the back they told him he would be given a reduced pension and that it was nothing personal.

He was shipwrecked. It was the first time I heard my dad cry. Dad was left feeling betrayed by the very people he had served so well for many years. The ones who promised to take care of him were the very ones to take advantage of him in his innocent devotion to them. He crumbled into a realm of insecurity and desperate depression. All that seemed solid and stable to him was destroyed. He believed that at his age he would never find work again. He was an innocent victim abused by the overwhelming power of people who discarded him when they were finished with him. He was defiled in every sense of the word.

Defilement and the ways to avoid it were a big part of the Old Testament laws. Anything that was defiled was not allowed to exist in God's presence. There were voluminous rules to keep things undefiled and even more as to how they might be cleansed. The Book of Leviticus is filled with such rules to stay clean. People who had defiling diseases like leprosy were separated out as unclean to prevent them from touching (thus defiling) anyone else. Anything that would not, or could not, be cleansed of defilement was thrown out of the camp so as not to contaminate anyone or anything else.

When people are used for someone else's personal gain or pleasure without regard for their own good, it is an abnormal use, or an "ab-use." When people are abused and discarded, they live under the influence of defilement. Tamar was "ab-used" by her half-brother, Amnon, then thrown out in the cold. She was no longer pure in her own estimation. She was unfit for normal human relationships. She was left a desolate victim living in her brother Absalom's house, her hopes of a productive life with marriage and children dashed.

The influence of defilement leaves an imprint on the emotions of the defiled. It is a unique combination of insecurity, hopelessness, and shame. A person living under the influence of defilement lives his life mourning in desolation of what was done to him and consequently fears any new intimacy.

Emotional Profile of Defilement

Betrayed, Confused

One of the key elements of defilement is that of betrayal. To be betrayed is to be abused by someone we know and trust. It may be parents, a pastor, a teacher, or a sibling. That is the factor that makes it most damaging. Not only is something precious taken from the abused, but their trust is destroyed at the same time, leaving them in a confused state.

My wife and I have ministered to people who have been abused by all the various people listed above. One instance of abuse that was particularly damaging happened at the hands of a church deacon. The abuse was one of talking in suggestive and very inappropriate ways to a teenage girl, as well as inappropriate touching, which left the young girl confused. The betrayal was so unconscionable that the girl blotted it from her memory for more than 20 years until it surfaced during a ministry session.

Perhaps the worst part of this type of betrayal is that many times no one believes the victim when the abuse is reported. I recall a case in which abuse happened to a young girl by a pastor who was a friend of the family. When the girl reported it to her parents, she was the one who got punished for saying such a thing. This leaves the victim feeling as though there is nowhere to go—no one to protect her who will understand. Consequently, anger and hurt are pushed below the surface, just waiting to erupt at a future time. And guaranteed…it will erupt.

Violated, Damaged

Tamar begged her brother not to violate her. To be violated is to be broken into some way; it's when someone crosses a line that should never be crossed. Violation occurs when clearly posted signs are ignored and the perpetrator disregards the law—like someone who chooses to break the speed limit or who doesn't fully halt at a stop sign. The main feeling of violation is one of someone forcing his way to a forbidden place. Such was the case with Amnon, who clearly thumbed his nose at the law of God and the welfare of his half-sister.

When we have been violated, we feel that nothing and no one is safe. Once someone has jumped over the fence, it is pretty hard to feel anything but shocked and unprotected. Abused people lose the sense of safety; they now know that the lines of respect and proper behaviors are lines that someone else may choose to ignore. The fence is broken down and flattened by the disregarding lust of another person.

I recall a recent session in which a young woman had been so abused that she couldn't close her eyes to pray. To close her eyes would require trusting that I would not harm her in some way. She had been violated by two family members from a young age. To add to the trauma, her own father, who enjoyed a prominent position in the community, did not believe her story. Instead he punished her, making her feel doubly unsafe. He did not want the tales of abuse to get out and considered his reputation to be more important than her safety. So the abuse continued.

Disgraced, Degraded

To feel *disgraced* is to believe that there is no grace for us. This particular word carries the sense of foolishness or degradation. To be degraded or disgraced is to feel that we somehow have descended to a lower rung on the ladder, that we are no longer precious or valuable. We feel that we have no rights.

Sometimes the feelings of degradation are so strong that the victim steps down to that lower rung and begins to act out his or her degradation. Many of those to whom we minister who lived in lifestyles of sexual perversion or drug abuse can trace their struggles back to the time when they were abused themselves. They reasoned that since they were damaged goods, they might as well live that way. They see themselves as lesser people.

Shameful, Dirty

Defilement leaves people with a feeling of being dirty or shameful in some way. Even though they are the ones who have been defiled, they somehow blame themselves. Tamar was concerned that her brother's turning her out would make it look as though she was the guilty party. She said, "Sending me away is greater than the other that you have done to me!" (2 Sam. 13:16b) She thought that somehow she would be seen as the guilty party.

Those who have been abused, particularly sexually, believe that they had something to do with the offense against them or that they could have prevented it somehow. Perhaps they believe themselves to have been foolish or stupid. My wife and I have ministered to women who were raped who later said, "It was my fault. I should have known better than to be in that place or with that person." Whatever the specific words they use, they somehow believe that the defilement reflects guilt and blame on them.

When we ministered to the young woman who couldn't close her eyes because of fear, a memory surfaced of that cruel violation. As we looked at a memory filled with abuse, the young girl shuddered and hyperventilated in terror. Her security was compromised by the very ones who should have made her feel safe. It was so horrible that I asked her for no details. The striking thing about the memory was that even though she was the one being abused, she said that she was bad, that she was dirty.

Tamar said, in effect, "How will I get rid of this shame that is on me?" (see 2 Sam. 13:13) As we said in an earlier chapter, shame becomes like a defiling mud that sticks to us, not allowing us to get close to God or anyone else. This is even more so with the person who feels defiled. The abuse perpetrated against Tamar—the abnormal use of her body by her own half-brother—would cling to her for the rest of her life with no way of getting free of it.

Ruined, Spoiled Goods

In perhaps the most telling statement of all, the biblical text informs us that Tamar was desolate in her brother Absalom's house. To be desolate is to be like a howling wasteland, like a ghost town being reclaimed by the desert as in the Old West. The songs that were once sung are heard no longer; the activity and bustle of life are no longer in evidence. We could easily replace the word *desolate* with *ruin*, which evokes a picture of the ancient dilapidated cities with walls crumbling and no hope of future life. This is the feeling that many people experience under the influence of defilement.

When someone has been abused and lives under the influence of defilement, the motion of their lives comes to a screeching halt. They believe themselves to be spoiled just as Tamar did, who tore the sleeves off her garment in a symbolic motion of the end of her innocence and life as she hoped it might be. All that seemed to be good and precious had gone bad like a carton of milk left out of the refrigerator.

The defiled live in a continuous state of mourning. Tamar threw ashes on herself as though they were the ashes of incinerated hope, and she walked about with her hand on her head bewailing her condition. Like Tamar, people who are under the influence of defilement live as though they are at their own funerals, gazing at pictures of their days of innocence. For them life is over and they can't see how the ruins of their lives can ever be inhabited again.

I recall again how my own father who, when he was forcibly retired in favor of younger men, felt as though he would never work again, that he would never live another purposeful day. He believed, like Tamar did, that his life was spoiled, that it had gone bad and would never again amount to anything. God, however, had other plans.

These and other feelings crop up to rob the defiled of intimacy with God. But God, who is faithful and compassionate, invites us back into His presence to heal our wounds and restore us.

The Truth About Defilement

During ministry, the young woman who had been molested by family members came to a place of terror on confronting the memory picture. It was so vivid and real to her, it was as though it might happen to her again. She said, "I was bad"; she said that it was her fault. But when we asked the Lord to show her the truth—what He believed about her and the abuse—He simply said, "I love you." It was all she needed to hear. It was proof that she was still precious and valuable. With that the hyperventilation and trembling stopped, as if turned off by a switch.

Once the trembling stopped, the Lord said, "This was not your fault; you are not bad."

With that the guilt and slime of shame was lifted off her. She was able to hear what the Lord was saying, and she was able to close her eyes to receive a blessing and the truth, which is our usual conclusion to the ministry session.

The Truth Is...It Is Not Your Fault

Note that we could not change history; she had been abused. But now she saw that the Lord had not left her alone. She was safe in His love. She found Someone to trust. With that, her defensiveness and distrust began to evaporate. She was safe in the embrace of God. The Torah is clear on whose sin the abuse is:

> But if in the field the man finds the girl who is engaged, and the man forces her and lies with her, then only the man who lies with her shall die. But you shall do nothing to the girl; there is no sin in the girl worthy of death, for just as a man rises against his neighbor and murders him, so is this case (Deuteronomy 22:25-26).

The truth is that you were the one sinned against. You did not participate of your own free will. There was probably little or nothing you could do to stop the attack. You trusted someone else who took advantage of that trust to satisfy his own need without regarding yours. The thought never occurred to Tamar that her own half-brother would rape her. She went into his room to minister to him and nothing else. It is perhaps true that her decision to go into the room provided an easier avenue for the perpetrator to commit the abuse, but she was in no way to blame for the sin of another person.

God Was With You

The most frequent opposition to healing in this scenario is the notion that God could not possibly have been there when we were abused. This is because we believe that the sin against us was too great or that somehow God just abandoned us to our abuser. Many times people who have been abused say there was no way that the Lord could have been there. If He loved them, why did He allow it to happen? The truth is, however, that God was there even in that place and that He never stopped loving them for a moment.

Time after time those to whom the Lord is ministering healing have sensed the presence of God around them. God never abandoned them to the abuser. He was there, and because God is not bound by time or dimension as we are, God would see the very day of their healing even as they were being abused. The truth is that people do bad things because they choose to; they have free will. But those bad things are never God's idea. God always leads us back to His embrace and healing, even from the greatest wounding.

Life Is Not Over

Although the following Scriptures apply to the nation of Israel, they also point to God's predisposition to heal and restore those who are living ruined lives. God desires to bring us back to Himself and into fruitful lives. Our lives are not over because of the sin of another person. As God heals us, we find a new life anchored in His healing presence and compassion. God will restore us to all that we ever were intended to be in Him.

> *Also I will restore the captivity of My people Israel, and they will rebuild the ruined cities and live in them; they will also plant vineyards and drink their wine, and make gardens and eat their fruit* (Amos 9:14).

For the Lord will restore the splendor of Jacob like the splendor of Israel, even though devastators have devastated them and destroyed their vine branches (Nahum 2:2).

(See the *Personal Ministry Guide* at the end of this book to process the issue of defilement.)

CHAPTER FOURTEEN

STARING INTO EMPTINESS

Hopelessness

But Mary was standing outside the tomb weeping; and so, as she wept, she stooped and looked into the tomb; and she saw two angels in white sitting, one at the head and one at the feet, where the body of Jesus had been lying. And they said to her, "Woman, why are you weeping?" She said to them, "Because they have taken away my Lord, and I do not know where they have laid Him" (John 20:11-13).

The Portrait of Hopelessness

She just couldn't sleep. She tossed and turned all night long thinking, wondering, weeping. Her Lord had delivered her from seven devils; He could open up the Word of God to her like none other. She had seen Him do many miracles—countless wonders among the desperate and poor. But the image that remained in her heart was that of His broken body as it hung from the rough wooden emblem of shame—a body that was now as cold and lifeless as the rock-hewn tomb to which it had been carried. Now what would become of her life? What kind of future could there be for a healed hooker? She had burned all her bridges to follow this Man. It was dark.

As the night wore on in a monotonous, stinging barrenness, the oil in the little clay lamp on the wall was running out. In her pain she had not bothered to refill it. As the light flickered with the last drop of oil, Mary looked outside the window of her little house and saw that the sky had gone from black to an indigo blue as dawn and the end of her troubled sleep were at hand.

The woman called Magdalene arose from her bed, which had been little help in giving sleep to her the night before. Though she respected the Sabbath, it had been more like a sentence than a time of rest. She could wait no longer to visit the tomb of her Lord. So Mary set out from her house in the predawn hour with a bundle of spices to finish the preparation of the body of Jesus.

As she drew near to the tomb in the dim of predawn, she was sure that her eyes, puffy and tired from her weeping, were playing tricks on her. Astonished to see that the large stone in front of the tomb had already been rolled away, Mary rushed to the mouth of the tomb carved into the rocky hillside and stooped over to look inside. As she gazed in, two angels in the form of young men sat there, one at the head and the other at the foot of where the body of Jesus had lain. Her mourning heart was prepared to see the body of her Lord, but it was not there.

Her restless and tired body now became alive with shock and conjecture. What had they done with the body of her crucified Lord? Wasn't it enough that they had whipped and mutilated Him while He was alive? Who would have taken away His lifeless body? The two angels on the empty slab looked into Mary's face with a restful calm and asked, "Why are you weeping?"

What a cruel and thoughtless question. "Someone has taken away my Lord," she answered with a sad resignation.

Mary was left stooped over and weeping at the empty tomb. All that she expected—all she had ever hoped in the great Man she followed—came to a pointless end in a cold and empty hole in the rock. She was staring into emptiness—the picture of hopelessness.

The Influence of Hopelessness

The lie that inspires hopelessness is "*I will never....*" You can fill in the rest of the sentence. For us, as with Mary, hope is the thing that keeps us moving forward toward some positive expectation. We hope that our children find good mates and settle down. We hope that the doctor's diagnosis is favorable. We hope that the stock market rises and carries our 401k plan with it. Our hope in any situation is for a positive outcome according to our understanding.

We can recognize the influence of hopelessness when we just want to sit down and quit. I saved my own story for this chapter since hopelessness and depression are my own issues. I have had seasons of staring into emptiness when nothing made sense and my life seemed to come to a senseless and confusing halt. I have just wanted to sit down and quit.

I spent most of my 30's building a retail music company. My wife and I bought a small company in the little town of Chambersburg, Pennsylvania, in 1983, investing all of our savings. The business grew well and in a few years was doing many times the sale volume that it did before we purchased it. Things seemed to be going well, and I began to see the flicker of a prosperous future just over the horizon.

Both Carol and I grew in our faith during those years, and that faith spilled over into the business. We paid our tithes and enjoyed intercession and a fair amount of ministry in the store. Things seemed to be moving along. By and large we were hopeful of a bright and secure future. But all was not well in musicland.

Eventually the bottom fell out of the music market, at least in the areas where we had invested our efforts. Within a couple years' time our growing business went south and we were broke. Finally, we went into bankruptcy and spent a year working for another dealer while at the same time trying to liquidate our business so as to keep our default to a minimum. We were able to pay off most of our debt and reorganize the rest, but we were devastated. All seemed bleak—and on top of it all, I was now 40. The questions on my mind then were, "Who will want a 40-year-old failure like me? How will I make a living?" My vision of the future barely reflected the limited revelation of God's plan that I did have.

That, however, was not the end of anything; it was only the beginning. After a few months my life totally changed. True, I was out of the music business that until then had been my life, but now I was in the arena of Christian publishing and headed toward full-time ministry. You see, while in the music business, I had taken a few courses at a nearby Bible college and studied Hebrew for a couple years with a local rabbi who became a close friend. That directed this new stage in my life, and it could not have been more different. I began to see that neither God's plan nor His love for me had ceased when we closed our store in failure. It was not the end; it was the beginning. God had been with me the whole time and is with me now as I write these words.

Hoping and seeing go together, but it is a seeing with the heart rather than with the eyes. Maybe we could call it "vision." The Bible tells us that we hope for what we do not see. If we saw it, we wouldn't have to hope for it; it would already be in our hands. (See Romans 8:24-25.) We would not hope for a raise in salary that we already had. But we might hope—we might dare to speculate on what we would do with that extra money if it was to come to us. Whatever we see ourselves doing with that extra money is what we hope for.

Hopelessness is the influence of the Jebusites, whose name may be interpreted as downtrodden or beaten down. When I think of the Jebusites, I see a people who excelled in dashing hopes and expectation. It was the Jebusites in Second Samuel chapter 5 who controlled the citadel of Jerusalem. As King David moved toward establishing his reign on Mount Zion, it was the Jebusites who told him he didn't have a prayer of doing so. They put their blind and lame on the walls to taunt him, saying, "You will never get in here." The words *hopeless* and *trampled* seem to fit well together.

Never is the operative word of hopelessness. We see only obstacles and no way to get around them. Hopelessness is taking the visible evidence, comparing it to what we know, and determining that we will never get there...we will never make it...never...never...never. Hopelessness is the belief that something is impossible, given our understanding of reality. For example, we look at our checkbook and then the bills, and we determine that—based upon our understanding and resources—there is no hope of paying all of them.

The universal response to hopelessness is to simply quit. It is as though we are in a rowboat moving into a fog. When we can no longer see ahead, we just give up and stop rowing. We sit in the fog and wait for something bad to happen. When we can't see or understand, we don't move ahead.

Hopelessness kills our desire for life. Many older people die for lack of vision and hope. They see nothing further they can do and despair of any further purpose in their lives. "Where there is no vision [no hope], the people perish" (Prov. 29:18a KJV). There is a blight on the senior population of our nation because we have been taught a retirement mentality. We not only retire from a job; we also retire from life and hope.

We hope for what we see. When we can no longer see, we no longer hope. We become hopeless.

Emotional Profile of Hopelessness

There are several emotions that flow out of hopelessness. When we are under the influence of hopelessness we feel...

Cursed, Doomed

"This just isn't going to go my way...Things will never work out...Nothing will ever change...Here we go again...." These are the words and feelings of the hopeless.

To feel cursed is to feel as though there is a heavy and inescapable weight of impending doom assigned to our lives, as though we are the children of a lesser God. We've seen this many times in the lives of those who have come out of prison—or even in their children, who believe that it is their lot in life to follow their parents to prison.

Once when I was visiting the warden of the local county jail, he told me that the children of those in prison were seven times more likely to find themselves there in the future. I'm not sure where he got his statistics, but he could rattle off several instances of multiple generations in his own prison. What's worse is that the children of the inmates in his prison naturally expected to be there; it became part of the culture of their futures. Such is the influence of hopelessness.

Hope-less-ness is exactly that: living under the curse of a lesser hope. I think of Mary Magdalene who was delivered from seven devils. (By the way, that is a Bible way of saying that she was completely bound by the enemy.) Imagine the emotion and the self-talk that flooded her heart as she looked into the empty tomb. "Here we go again...I was never really free...I have nowhere else to go." It was a feeling that left her stooped over and weeping at an empty tomb.

Defeated

When we live under the influence of hopelessness, we live with the white flag of surrender raised over us. We have surely been defeated and the only thing left for us to do is to work out the terms of unconditional surrender to a lesser life and a lesser hope. As a result, we walk around with heads hung as low as our expectations.

When we give in to feelings of defeat, we play into the enemy's hands. He wants us to believe that we have been beaten, that he is stronger. David talks about the taunts of his enemies over his own life and reign:

A Psalm of David, when he fled from Absalom his son.

O Lord, how my adversaries have increased! Many are rising up against me. Many are saying of my soul, "There is no deliverance for him in God" (Psalm 3:1-2).

It is not hard to feel defeated when the casualties begin to pile up around us. When we have tried our hardest and still get nothing better than C's on our report card; when we have given all the love we've got and our spouse still chooses adultery—we feel as though the battle is over and all hope is lost. At that point our flag is fallen and the enemy has his way with us. However, to be sure, it is not the end of the story!

Indifferent, Resigned

Many who cannot see hope for tomorrow simply stop looking for it. They stay within the confines of their limited perspectives. There is a feeling that life exceeds their grasp, that every time their hand is on the doorknob of opportunity it will not turn. The result is that sooner or later they just stop reaching and quit.

Those who have lived under hopelessness resign in every sense of the word. They quit. They think that there is no reason to go on since they will fail anyway. Their hope becomes calloused and they become indifferent; they no longer care. Again, they are the image of Mary weeping at an empty tomb. A hole in the ground has little hope or motivation to move us forward. Therefore, we just stop moving.

Pessimistic, Negative

Once we have stopped moving, we begin to see everything as futile. We become missionaries of hopelessness and see the world in a negative light. Nothing will ever work out; nothing will ever be the same again. We become like Eeyore, the little stuffed donkey in the Winnie the Pooh stories. For him, life was the sound of the other shoe falling. There was no use looking forward to anything because life just doesn't work out, and that's the way it is.

There is a supreme irony in the scene of Mary before the empty tomb. The very thing that should have encouraged her—an empty tomb—was the thing that made her feel hopeless. If she had had a proper revelation of what Jesus always said He was going to do, she would have rejoiced at the fact that He had risen. But Mary looked at the empty tomb with human understanding, and instead of jumping for joy, she was sad.

Pessimism and negativity are the result of our woefully deficient human understanding. We take what we have learned in the past—our own experience and understanding—and we predict the future. To Mary an empty tomb meant a missing body rather than a resurrected Lord. She was left with no thought that Jesus was more than she thought He was. Her view of the future and her hope of ever seeing Jesus again was dashed. Her best hope now was to find her dead Rabbi and give His body a decent burial. New revelation was standing right behind her all the time, though. She just didn't recognize it. Neither do we when we are living under the influence of hopelessness.

Disappointed, Empty

Sometimes we spend our time dreaming and expecting things that do not happen. We might say that we *appoint* something to happen. Then, when it doesn't, we become dis-appointed from that expectation. We are separated from our vision. Perhaps a woman dreams all her life of having and holding her own baby. She sees herself nursing and loving a tiny gift of precious life. Then the doctor finds an abnormality that makes it difficult for her to have children. What she has dreamed of all her life may never happen as she has seen it. All that she has hoped for may never come to fruition. She becomes as Mary was, staring into emptiness. The thing entombed was her hope, which is now dead in its absence.

There are many cases where spouses wrap their lives around their mates, acquiring their entire significance from that marriage—only to have that spouse die or leave. That absence then creates a giant, life-sucking vacuum that draws everything into it. These spouses may try to fill the emptiness with activity, or they may try to fill it with denial. But in the end, they are left with a hole that can never be filled. To be sure, the greatest disappointment is caused because their expectations are too high, or they are too consumed with the marriage and less grounded in God. Whatever the reason, the hopeless are left feeling grieved, disappointed, and empty.

Depressed

Perhaps the most pronounced emotion under the influence of hopelessness is depression. Depression is the feeling that we are standing on the precipice of a bottomless pit and cannot seem to find the energy to move back from the edge. There seems to be no way out and nowhere to go but over the edge. The only vision we have is of ourselves falling through the empty blackness, waiting for the inevitable destruction.

I must admit that I have felt defeated many times in ministry. There are those to whom we don't seem to be able to bring healing. The ones we love the most—the ones we invest the most in—are sometimes the most difficult to minister to. Perhaps this is why the Lord grants us an extra measure of love for them.

Many times I have felt as though I am staring into a deep, dark, and empty hole whose dimensions threaten to swallow up my life and ministry. I cannot see how anything I have done or could ever do might bring healing to severely abused or disturbed people. I love them, but in that love I feel helpless and lost. In a word, I am depressed.

Depression is a common problem in our society today with many people taking antidepressant drugs. It seems that every other person we meet is on Prozac. Life for these people has gotten so complicated, so black, that they have lost all vision in the ever-increasing tangles of worry, children, career, world tensions, retirement plans, and all the rest. They are caught on the horns of hopelessness with little thought of anything ever working out.

All of these—doom, defeat, indifference, resignation, pessimism, emptiness, depression, and disappointment—are the fruit of hopelessness. They are formidable obstacles to moving forward into the abundance of God. All of them are the product of limited revelation of the Person and work of Jesus Christ. But there is a greater revelation coming that leads us to the truth about hope.

The Truth About Hopelessness

When she had said this, **she turned around and saw Jesus standing there, and did not know that it was Jesus.** *Jesus said to her,* **"Woman, why are you weeping? Whom are you seeking?"** *Supposing Him to be the gardener, she said to Him, "Sir, if you have carried Him away, tell me where you have laid Him, and I will take Him away."* **Jesus said to her, "Mary!" She turned and said to Him in Hebrew, "Rabboni!"** *(which means, Teacher). Jesus said to her, "Stop clinging to Me, for I have not yet ascended to the Father; but go to My brethren and say to them, 'I ascend to My Father and your Father, and My God and your God.'"* *Mary Magdalene came, announcing to the disciples,* **"I**

have seen the Lord," *and that He had said these things*
to her (John 20:14-18, emphasis added).

As Mary was stooped over and weeping into the emptiness,
she became aware of a presence at her back. Turning around mo-
mentarily from her dark focus, she saw what appeared to be the
gardener, the one in charge of the cemetery. No sooner had His
appearing interrupted her grief than He asked her the same
thoughtless question the angels had: "Why are you weeping?"
But then He added, "Whom are you seeking?"

In her tortured disappointment she thought that perhaps He
had carried the body of her Lord away. After all, it was a borrowed tomb. Maybe the owner wanted it back. She said to the gardener, "Please tell me where You have put His body. I'll carry
Him to another tomb."

Just then, as she was turning her attention back to the emptiness, the figure behind her, whose presence she had felt, spoke
one word. "Mary!" He spoke as if to awaken her from the slumber of inadequate revelation. "Mary!" She was awakened as from
a dead sleep by a voice that resonated against her deepest hope.
Her mind was overwhelmed by her thrilled heart. Something like
scales fell from her eyes as she recognized the identity of the
presence that had been behind her. Now, fully and finally turned
around, she said, "My Master!"

Jesus had gone from Lord to her *LORD*.

As she spoke these words, she grabbed onto the hem of His
garment, but the risen Lord said, "Don't hang onto Me, or onto
who you think I am. Instead, go and tell the others who have not
seen Me who I really am."

With that Mary ran to the others who loved Jesus and said,
"I have really seen the *LORD*."

Our Hope Is Alive

In her grief at the empty tomb, Mary missed something that
we might observe 2,000 years later. There were two angels, one
sitting at the head and one at the foot of the place where the body
of Jesus had been laid. They were "sitting." Why? Because there

was nothing else to be done. Everything was under control. They were not concerned as she was. For a moment, those angels had a greater revelation of Jesus, who was more than a dead itinerant rabbi. He was the Lord of life, the eternal One, the Creator. He was alive! "Blessed be the God and Father of our Lord Jesus Christ, who according to His great mercy has caused us to be *born again to a living hope* through the resurrection of Jesus Christ from the dead" (1 Pet. 1:3, emphasis added).

We humans tend to see our lives in a static plan of action and reaction, of sequence and consequence. "For we know in part and we prophesy in part" (1 Cor. 13:9). The reality is that while things may seem hopeless according to our understanding, they are very much intact in God's view. The problem is that we just do not see it.

Get this picture. While Mary was standing stooped over, staring into the emptiness, Jesus was standing right behind her all the time. While she was seeing the end of her hope and vision, the presence of God was practically breathing down her neck. She did not see Him at first because of her disappointed expectations. But there He was, alive and inviting her to see Him.

What was required in order for Mary to see her living hope was that she turn around. To turn around from a Hebrew perspective is to repent, from the word *shuv*. This means that we move in a new direction. How many times are we staring into emptiness when all the time the Lord is standing behind us? The Lord Himself is right there speaking our name and rousing us from our *focus on circumstances*. All we have to do is turn around to see Him.

Our hope is based more on what we can't see than on what we can see. "For in hope we have been saved, but hope that is seen is not hope; for who hopes for what he already sees? But if we hope for what we do not see, with perseverance we wait eagerly for it" (Rom. 8:24-25).

When we are suffocating under the influence of hopelessness, we need to ask God to enable us to see Him. So often we consider His presence for a moment, then turn back to the emptiness. That is why our Christian lives seem to jerk from one crisis to the next—or from one miracle to the next.

As we consistently see the presence of the living Christ, we find hope that won't disappear with the next overdraft notice from the bank. We find hope that won't fade away with our looks (for those of us who have looks, that is). We will approach even the most hopeless situation with eagerness to see the presence of God revealed. We have a living hope.

Our Hope Is in a Person

Jesus not only asked Mary, "Why are you weeping?" but also "Whom are you seeking?" Mary came to the tomb seeking an "it," not a "whom." She came expecting to find a body, a deceased shell of a great teacher and miracle worker.

There is a connection between what we seek—what we are focused on—and what we feel. What we feel comes from what we believe or trust. Therefore, Mary must have believed that Jesus was a great Rabbi, a compassionate healer, a kindly and personable friend, but she did not believe Him to be the Lord. Her hope ended at the mouth of the tomb.

In reality, Mary, the one who loved and followed Jesus so closely, had no greater revelation and hope than did the Pharisees and priests who crucified Him. They asked that guards be placed around the tomb so that His followers could not take His body and claim that He had risen from the dead (see Mt. 27:64). Mary also believed that someone had carried off the body of Jesus.

Our hope is found in a greater revelation of Jesus Christ. Mary followed Jesus for at least a couple of years, but despite her closeness to Him, she was still hopeless.

She had been delivered of seven devils—she was still hopeless.

She had heard the teaching—she was still hopeless.

She had seen countless miracles—she was still hopeless.

She was at the foot of the cross when Jesus spoke—she was still hopeless.

She saw an empty tomb—she was still hopeless.

She saw the angels—she was still hopeless.

None of it made sense to her. It was not real; it was not personal. She remained, despite the great teaching and deliverance, ignorant of the truth of Jesus and in her despair. She was hopeless because she hoped *for* something less than the risen Christ. It isn't wrong to hope *for* something, but our hope must be *in* God Himself. We can hope for healing, but healing cannot be our hope. We can hope for financial security, but financial security cannot be our hope. Our hope is in the character of a good and faithful God, in a risen and powerful *LORD*.

It is not what we know—it is not what we see in other lives or in miracles—but our personal revelation of Jesus and the experiencing of His personal intimacy that heals us from hopelessness. "And now, Lord, for what do I wait? My hope is in You" (Ps. 39:7).

It is here where Jesus and the grace of God become real to us. This is where we bring our lives under the reality of His presence. This is where we turn the corner in our faith and experience the dynamic reality of our lives in Christ. This was the place where Mary's personal knowledge of Jesus went from Lord to *her personal LORD*.

As we turn toward God, we see Him as He is and purify ourselves from what is not real. "And everyone who has this hope fixed on Him purifies himself, just as He is pure" (1 Jn. 3:3). The character of God is the collateral of our hope. We have cause to hope even in the bleakest of circumstances, even if things don't work out to our understanding. Why? Because in the end God is good. In eternity He will be glorified in our defeats and failures as much as or more than in our apparent triumphs.

For those living under the influence of hopelessness, this is an invitation from the living God to turn away from staring into the emptiness and turn toward Him. He is here, behind you even now, speaking your name.

(See the *Personal Ministry Guide* at the end of this book to process the issue of hopelessness.)

PART THREE

WALKING IN THE TRUTH

CHAPTER FIFTEEN

TO BE CONTINUED...

The Lord your God will clear away these nations be-
fore you little by little; you will not be able to put an
end to them quickly, for the wild beasts would grow too
numerous for you (Deuteronomy 7:22).

The healing work has begun in you. Now you must walk
through and take possession of your inheritance "little by little."
The Lord has led you to the source of your pain and brought
truth, order, and peace to your heart. He has replaced lies with
truth and given you a new awareness of His presence and His loving intentions toward you. But the healing work goes on—it is *to*
be continued.

Our healing continues as we walk closer to the Lord and
find more Truth—more of Jesus Christ—more of the abundant
life He has purchased for us. All healing and truth converge at the
cross of Christ. Our healing now continues to pervade every aspect of our lives to dethrone every fear and every thought that ex-
alts itself against the knowledge (truth) of God. We take every
thought captive as we obey and turn toward the voice of the One
who loves and accepts us (see 2 Cor. 10:3-5).

New Ruts

Roy Kreider, my mentor in inner healing, taught me that we
tend to live in ruts worn by habits and routine. Roy, who grew up
in Lancaster County, Pennsylvania, uses the image of a horse-
drawn wagon returning to the barn at the end of the day. When a
wagon has been on the same path many times, it digs deep ruts in
the dirt. The well-worn ruts in the earth then provide a kind of
guide or track that guide the wheels of the wagon. As long as the
farmer can get the wagon in the ruts, he can just slap the horses

on the rump, send them on their way to the barn, and not even have to drive the wagon.

You and I have worn ruts in the landscape of our minds and hearts. There are patterns established in our lives and understanding that carry us to the barn, so to speak. Even when we have received truth and healing, those ruts are still there and our lives run into them. The solution is to continue to walk—to live—new truths and follow a new path that always leads us to Jesus.

We quoted the prophet Isaiah in an earlier chapter where he said, "You will see your teacher with your own eyes, and you will hear a voice say, 'This is the way; turn around and walk here' " (Is. 30:20b-21 NLT). As you have journeyed through this book, you did indeed meet your Teacher and hear His voice. His voice has caused you to turn in a new direction—to repent from old thinking and ruts and find the true way to Him and healing. Now that you have heard and turned toward the presence of the Lord Jesus, you must continue to walk toward Him.

Jesus told those who followed Him to *continue* to walk in the new paths He had provided for them—paths that would lead to more and more freedom.

> *So Jesus was saying to those Jews who had believed Him, "If you continue in My word, then you are truly disciples of Mine; and you will know the truth, and the truth will make you free"* (John 8:31-32).

Jesus said that it was not enough to hear the truth; we need to continue to walk it out, to make it part of our lives. Even when we have heard the truth and believed it, we can still fall into the familiar ruts and patterns that have carried us through life. It is as we continue to walk in the truth that He speaks to us that we come to know it by experience and wear new ruts of righteousness in our lives that lead us to Him.

All healing and all truth converge at the cross of Christ. It was at the cross that all the lies and ruts of Eden's fall were eliminated and a new path provided. The way of the cross leads to intimacy with God Himself through the atoning work of Christ. If separation from the presence of God is the root of all emotional pain—and it is—then union with God in Christ is the healing for it. In His presence there is fullness of joy...healing...peace... abundant life.

As we close this part of the book, I want to give you some new and "righteous ruts" to follow. Allow the truth of the Word to lead you to the fount of all healing: Jesus Christ. Read these words in the presence of God and follow the Teacher's voice to the source. When you are afraid, or whenever your wheels seem to find those old ruts that were so automatic, declare these truths and allow yourself to see them unfold before your lives. You have new promises in the presence of Jesus Christ.

The Healing Truth

- ### *Fear—You Are Not Alone.*

  Behold, I am with you and will keep you wherever you go, and will bring you back to this land; for I will not leave you until I have done what I have promised you (Genesis 28:15).

  Be strong and courageous, do not be afraid or tremble at them, for the Lord your God is the one who goes with you. He will not fail you or forsake you (Deuteronomy 31:6).

  Have I not commanded you? Be strong and coura- geous! Do not tremble or be dismayed, for the Lord your God is with you wherever you go (Joshua 1:9).

  The Lord of hosts is with us; the God of Jacob is our stronghold (Psalm 46:7).

  Be strong and courageous, do not fear or be dismayed because of the king of Assyria nor because of all the horde that is with him; for the one with us is greater than the one with him (2 Chronicles 32:7).

  But now, thus says the Lord, your Creator, O Jacob, and He who formed you, O Israel, "Do not fear, for I have redeemed you; I have called you by name; you are Mine! When you pass through the waters, I will be with you; and through the rivers, they will not overflow you.

*When you walk through the fire, you will not be
scorched, nor will the flame burn you"* (Isaiah 43:1-2).

- ### Rejection—You Are Accepted in Christ.

  *They will say of Me, "Only in the Lord are righteous-
  ness and strength." Men will come to Him, and all who
  were angry at Him will be put to shame. In the Lord all
  the offspring of Israel will be justified and will glory*
  (Isaiah 45:24-25).

  *In His days Judah will be saved, and Israel will dwell
  securely; and this is His name by which He will be
  called, "The Lord our righteousness"* (Jeremiah 23:6).

  *For all have sinned and fall short of the glory of God,
  being justified as a gift by His grace through the redemption which is in Christ Jesus* (Romans 3:23-24).

  *For the kingdom of God is not eating and drinking, but
  righteousness and peace and joy in the Holy Spirit. For
  he who in this way serves Christ is acceptable to God
  and approved by men* (Romans 14:17-18).

  *Having predestined us to adoption as sons by Jesus
  Christ to Himself, according to the good pleasure of
  His will, to the praise of the glory of His grace, by
  which He has made us accepted in the Beloved* (Ephesians 1:5-6 NKJ).

- ### Worthlessness—You Are Approved in Christ, Handmade and Precious.

  *God created man in His own image, in the image of
  God He created him; male and female He created them*
  (Genesis 1:27).

  *Know that the Lord Himself is God; it is He who has
  made us, and not we ourselves; we are His people and
  the sheep of His pasture* (Psalm 100:3).

  *Your hands made me and fashioned me; give me un-
  derstanding, that I may learn Your commandments*
  (Psalm 119:73).

For You formed my inward parts; You wove me in my mother's womb. I will give thanks to You, for I am fearfully and wonderfully made; wonderful are Your works, and my soul knows it very well (Psalm 139:13-14).

The people whom I formed for Myself will declare My praise (Isaiah 43:21).

But by the grace of God I am what I am... (1 Corinthians 15:10).

Therefore if anyone is in Christ, he is a new creature; the old things passed away; behold, new things have come (2 Corinthians 5:17).

For we are His workmanship, created in Christ Jesus for good works, which God prepared beforehand so that we would walk in them (Ephesians 2:10).

Do not lie to one another, since you laid aside the old self with its evil practices, and have put on the new self who is being renewed to a true knowledge according to the image of the One who created him (Colossians 3:9-10).

- ***Shame—You Are Clothed With Christ.***

How blessed is he whose transgression is forgiven, whose sin is covered! (Psalm 32:1)

For all of you who were baptized into Christ have clothed yourselves with Christ (Galatians 3:27).

I will rejoice greatly in the Lord, my soul will exult in my God; for He has clothed me with garments of salvation, He has wrapped me with a robe of righteousness (Isaiah 61:10a).

But put on the Lord Jesus Christ, and make no provision for the flesh in regard to its lusts (Romans 13:14).

- **Insecurity—You Are Safe in Christ.**

  The eternal God is a dwelling place, and underneath are the everlasting arms (Deuteronomy 33:27a).

  O Lord, how my adversaries have increased! Many are rising up against me. Many are saying of my soul, "There is no deliverance for him in God." Selah. But You, O Lord, are a shield about me, my glory, and the One who lifts my head (Psalm 3:1-3).

  Many are the sorrows of the wicked, but he who trusts in the Lord, lovingkindness shall surround him (Psalm 32:10).

  The angel of the Lord encamps around those who fear Him, and rescues them (Psalm 34:7).

  The Lord is your **keeper***; the Lord is your shade on your right hand. The sun will not smite you by day, nor the moon by night. The Lord will* **protect** *you from all evil; He will* **keep** *your soul. The Lord will* **guard** *your going out and your coming in from this time forth and forever* (Psalm 121:5-8, emphasis added).

  Those who trust in the Lord are as Mount Zion, which cannot be moved but abides forever. As the mountains surround Jerusalem, so the Lord surrounds His people from this time forth and forever (Psalm 125:1-2).

  My sheep hear My voice, and I know them, and they follow Me; and I give eternal life to them, and they will never perish; and no one will snatch them out of My hand. My Father, who has given them to Me, is greater than all; and no one is able to snatch them out of the Father's hand (John 10:27-29).

- **Defilement—You Are Restored in Christ.**

  O God, restore us and cause Your face to shine upon us, and we will be saved (Psalm 80:3).

"For I will restore you to health and I will heal you of your wounds," declares the Lord, "because they have called you an outcast, saying: 'It is Zion; no one cares for her' " (Jeremiah 30:17).

"Then I passed by you and saw you, and behold, you were at the time for love; so I spread My skirt over you and covered your nakedness. I also swore to you and entered into a covenant with you so that you became Mine," declares the Lord God (Ezekiel 16:8).

Also I will restore the captivity of My people Israel, and they will rebuild the ruined cities and live in them; they will also plant vineyards and drink their wine, and make gardens and eat their fruit (Amos 9:14).

For the Lord will restore the splendor of Jacob like the splendor of Israel, even though devastators have devastated them and destroyed their vine branches (Nahum 2:2).

- ### *Hopelessness—You Have a Living Hope in Christ.*

O Israel, hope in the Lord; for with the Lord there is lovingkindness, and with Him is abundant redemption (Psalm 130:7).

For in hope we have been saved, but hope that is seen is not hope; for who hopes for what he already sees? But if we hope for what we do not see, with perseverance we wait eagerly for it (Romans 8:24-25).

Blessed be the God and Father of our Lord Jesus Christ, who according to His great mercy has caused us to be born again to a living hope through the resurrection of Jesus Christ from the dead, to obtain an inheritance which is imperishable and undefiled and will not fade away, reserved in heaven for you, who are protected by the power of God through faith for a salvation ready to be revealed in the last time (1 Peter 1:3-5).

Therefore, prepare your minds for action, keep sober in spirit, fix your hope completely on the grace to be brought to you at the revelation of Jesus Christ (1 Peter 1:13).

And everyone who has this hope fixed on Him purifies himself, just as He is pure (1 John 3:3).

There are many other Scriptures that could be added to these. I urge you to search them out. Read His words and allow them to draw you into His presence. Hear His voice and know Him.

The Beginning...

"For I am confident of this very thing, that He who began a good work in you will perfect it until the day of Christ Jesus" (Phil. 1:6). He has begun this work and drawn you into His presence to unveil His heart for you—to speak of His love for you. Continue in His Word and His love, listening for the sound of a gentle stilling as He speaks truth and peace to your heart. I encourage you to read and reread this book many times. Wear it out. Weep into it. Write down what the Lord speaks to you. He is speaking to you, even now, as you read these words. He is leading you to a new place of abundant, overflowing life in His presence.

Beloved, I whisper softly this invitation to you. I am thinking of you and praying for you as I echo these words spoken so long ago and that are still true for you today:

...the Lord longs to pour out His healing oil on you, to be gracious to you; He waits on high to demonstrate His intimate love for you. The Lord Himself will bless and reward your longing for Him with His presence (Isaiah 30:18, author's paraphrase).

Amen—Let it be so in Christ Jesus!

HEALING THE WOUNDED HEART PERSONAL MINISTRY GUIDE

Removing Obstacles to Intimacy With God

CONTENTS

INTRODUCTION

The Personal Ministry Guide is designed to help you, the reader, experience healing for areas of personal wounding that currently bring limitation in your life. Though one or more areas may be more prominent than others, it is recommended that you process through each of the influences we have presented in this book. It is necessary to continue to walk in the Truth the Lord reveals to you by also completing the journaling exercises provided at the end of each ministry session.

Throughout the following pages you will be dealing with the influences that have come into your life by various means. These are the influences of *fear, rejection, worthlessness, shame, insecurity, defilement,* and *hopelessness.* You are not bound by the outlines and suggested prayers in the next sections; but instead, respond to the *presence* of the Lord who longs to be gracious to you. Keep His face ever before you. Remember that it is the *presence* of God that brings healing, not the *process.*

To that end, each healing session begins with an exercise that will bring you to the face of God who longs to heal you. *"Therefore the Lord longs to be gracious to you, and therefore He waits on high to have compassion on you"* (Is. 30:18). You may assume that it's hard to see the face of God when you are dealing with some issues, but the presence of God is not determined by your issues; it is a fact. He is here and has been everywhere you have ever been. On the day of your wounding He was already moving you toward the day of your healing—today! There is nowhere you can go to be separated from the presence or face of God. *"Where can I go from Your Spirit? Or where can I flee from Your presence?"* (Ps. 139:7) The Lord who created you has invited you to a season of healing in His personal presence. As you respond to the gentle calling of the Father's heart, know that He is already waiting in a healing place to become and speak the truth to your heart and bring you peace.

Note that we have provided seven healing sessions based on the seven influences listed in Deuteronomy chapter 7. In fact, there may be a blending of these influences. Follow the Spirit of God into healing and not the process. Each healing session may take a few sittings. Again, be patient and follow the Spirit of God.

I pray the Lord who has invited you to this season of wholeness will bless you as you experience His healing presence.

THE INFLUENCE OF FEAR

PRAY THIS PRAYER ALOUD

Lord, I acknowledge that You have been present with me every moment of my life and that You desire to remove the influence of fear from my life. I acknowledge that fear sometimes causes me to turn from Your face and run away. I trust Your heart concerning me, that You want me to enjoy the abundant life and peace You have purchased for me in Christ. I declare that this time in Your presence is holy ground purchased by the blood of Jesus Christ. Therefore, I forbid any distracting influence. I now quiet my mind and choose to focus the eyes of my heart on Your face, trusting You to reveal the source of my fear. In Your name and presence, Lord Jesus, I pray. Amen.

FOCUSING ON THE PRESENCE OF GOD

Do you remember reading about Elijah as He hid in the cave paralyzed in fear? The Lord spoke to him in the midst of his fear with a gentle stilling sound. Now close your eyes and allow your heart to hear that "Shhhhh" sound from the very mouth of God that cuts through every interfering thought. Allow the other distractions to melt away into the sound of God's gentle stilling. Do not go any further until you have begun to experience the presence of the Lord. "Shhhhh."

UNCOVERING THE INFLUENCE OF FEAR

When does fear control you? Think of a recent or typical event when you felt alone and afraid—a time when your heart was telling you to run or avoid a person or circumstance. Close your eyes and focus on the recent or typical event.

Take a few minutes to write a brief description of the event in the space below. What made you want to run or avoid this person or circumstance? Remember that you are still safe in the presence of the Lord as you recall the fear-filled scene.

Describe what you were feeling during this event and how you reacted to those feelings. What did you do or want to do to react to this event? If there were any physical sensations associated with this event, make sure to write them down as well (e.g., sweating, accelerated heart rate, pain of any kind, etc.).

Now, pray that the Lord would lead you to the source of those feelings and sensations you experienced during that recent event. The memory He invites you into may look very different from the recent event, but the feelings and reactions will be the same.

Prayer: *Lord, I acknowledge Your presence in every season of my life and that You know where fear was planted and began to control my heart. I acknowledge that You are still alive in that place and ask You now to invite me there. I declare that I am safe in Your presence even as You lead me to healing. Amen.*

Wait for the Lord to show you where fear began to control your heart. (Note that there may be more than one memory. Try to determine the memory that stands out the most. Later you will process all the memories brought to light.) The Lord does not always lead us to the first memory but a memory that is most vivid and where He can most easily communicate truth.

Once the Lord has invited you to a memory, it is very important to stand back a few steps and look at it as though you were looking at a painting or a picture in a frame on the wall in front of you. This is important so that you are not so emotionally enmeshed that you cannot experience the presence of the Lord. Be intentional about taking steps back from the memory frame.

Now, describe what you see happening in the picture. (Remember to step back away from the picture.)

As you look into the memory frame, focus on the wounded child in the picture (you at that time). What does that wounded child in the picture feel? Include any physical sensations he/she may have experienced as well. Note things like the posture of the wounded child and his/her general appearance. Describe the child you see in front of you as fully as you can. What does the child in the picture want to do as a result of what is happening and what is he/she feeling as a result? (I remind you again to stand away from the picture and look at it as if looking into a picture frame or perhaps through a window to see the event in front of you.)

Now, why does the child feel what he feels? (The "why" is the lie he believes that causes the fear.)

"The child in the picture (you at that time) feels _____ because he believes: _____
_____
_____ .

(EXPERIENCING THE PRESENCE OF GOD)

Prayer: *Lord, by faith I acknowledge Your presence in my pain and ask You to express Your personal presence and heart to comfort the wounded child in the memory frame You have led me to. In Your presence I command all other false voices to silence, and I declare Your sovereign authority over my life. I now wait in Your presence for Your healing truth.*

Describe how you experience the presence of the Lord (i.e., feelings, impressions, images, actions the Lord may take, etc.). This is an act of faith, not imagination. One way to do this is to see the memory frame as a painting with the Lord painting His presence into the scene. You may see an image of the Lord or some other expression of His personal presence. What do you see or sense in the frame? How do you know His presence is there? What is He doing—saying—expressing—gesturing to you as you focus on Him? Again, stand back from the picture frame so that you can see what is happening in front of you.

What does the Lord seem to be communicating to the wounded child in the frame? How do you sense the personal presence of the Lord comforting the wounded child? How do you feel the Lord's interaction with you in a physical sense? Take time to experience the personal presence of the Lord in the memory frame feeling the warmth of His touch or the fragrance of His sweetness. Connect with His presence—body, soul, and spirit. Allow the presence of the Lord to comfort the wounded child in the memory. Is there anything else you sense the Lord communicating?

DECLARING THE TRUTH

What is the truth about this situation that the Lord is communicating through the expression of His presence, words, feelings, pictures, etc.?

- **Declaration of Truth:** "I felt *fear* because I believed

_____

_____

_____ .

But the truth is [whatever you sense the Lord communicating to that wounded child in the frame] _____

_____

_____ .

I now renounce the lie(s) I came to believe and declare the truth that _____

_____

_____ .

Now that you have received the truth of God, you must "change the locks" so that fear can no longer move back in to control your life. You "change the locks" by breaking any promises you have made to yourself as a wounded child and by extending forgiveness and removing judgments you have held against those who wounded you.

CHANGING THE LOCKS

Renouncing Self-promises

Prayer: *"Lord, I confess to You that I made a promise to myself when I was wounded that I would/would not _____*

_____ . I now break that

promise I made to myself because the truth is _____

_____

_____

Now that I have broken the promise I made to myself, I give You control of my heart and life."

Extending Forgiveness

To be free of the influence of fear, you must forgive or receive forgiveness associated with the memory. Forgive and release judgments you have held against those who've wounded you. (Remember that forgiveness is not an act of emotion, but an act of the will so that the pain of that memory can no longer control you.) Speak to them as though you and they are still in that old memory frame. Confess and receive forgiveness for any sin you are responsible for.

> **Prayer:** *Lord, I pray that You bring to my mind any person who I have held judgment or bitterness against because of this wounding event. I choose to see them and myself with Your eyes of compassion and to release any judgment I have held in my heart.*

To receive forgiveness yourself pray...

> **Prayer:** *"Lord, I confess* [any sin you may have committed in the memory the Lord invited you into]. *In this sin I gave legal ground to the enemy of my soul. I now receive forgiveness in the name of Jesus Christ who took this and all my sins upon Himself. I ask You to remove the effects of my sin and restore me to Your presence again.*

To extend mercy and forgiveness, pray...

> **Prayer:** *Lord,* [name the one who wounded you], [tell the Lord what this person or persons did to wound you]. *This wounding caused me to believe* [whatever the lie was that you renounced above] *and to feel* [what the wounded child felt in the memory frame]. *But now, in the presence of the Lord Jesus Christ, I extend grace and forgiveness to them and choose to see them with compassion as You see them.*

Now that you are safe in the presence of the Lord and wrapped in the truth, pause for a moment and look at those who

have wounded you. How do you see them as you bask in the presence of God? What is the truth about them?

I remove all judgments I have held against those who have wounded me and see them as children of God. The truth the Lord has spoken about those who have wounded me is _____

_____

_____.

Remove demonic strongholds

Declaration: *"Now that I have heard and believe the truth of God which is* [whatever was communicated to the wounded child in the memory frame], *and have forgiven those who wounded me and have removed all judgments I held against them and broken the promise(s) I made to myself; I command all evil and dark spirits who have held lies, judgments, and self-promises in place to depart from me and from my house. You have no legal ground on which to stand.*

Prayer: *Lord, I ask You to now reveal to me any other legal ground I have given to the enemy on which to stand.* [Listen to your heart carefully to see whether or not the Lord may reveal other unfinished business related to this wounding.]

Now ask the Lord to invite you into any other memories with the same feelings and lies, and repeat the process above with each one. You may want to use a separate notebook in which to record these additional memories and the truth the Lord speaks to you in this healing session.

CONTINUING IN THE TRUTH

Now that you have received Truth and healing in the presence of God, it is important to understand that this is only the beginning of healing. Healing is not magical; it is a process. You must continue in the truth and carve new "righteous ruts" for your heart to live in. Refer now to the biblical truths for the various issues in the chapter called "To Be Continued." You may also want to refer to some other topical Bible source to find additional biblical truths that can be applied to your life.

1. Choose a verse from the section "The Healing Truth" relating to fear in Chapter 15 that stands out to you. Write that verse in the space below.

2. Meditate on the statements. Read the verse several times aloud until you can close your eyes, repeat the Word, and see what the Word is saying to you.[1]

3. As you begin to see this Scripture text in your mind, focus on the presence of the Lord as you sense Him in the Word.

4. Experience the truth in this Scripture, watching and listening for any additional things the Lord may communicate to you personally. You are not changing or adding to the Word but allowing the Lord to continue the conversation.

---

1.   To meditate on the Word, is literally to murmur (from the Hebrew word *hagah*) or repeat the Word or the truth of God to ourselves in a low voice.

5. Now write down/journal whatever you sense is being communicated to you from the Lord in the Scripture text.

6. Repeat the steps above with additional verses from Chapter 15, section "The Healing Truth; Fear—You Are Not Alone."

What to Do if Fear Is Triggered Again

1. Go back to the healed memory frame to experience the presence of the Lord.

2. Remind the child in the picture of the presence and the truth of the Lord.

3. Meditate on the scriptural truths that stood out to you, repeating them until you can close your eyes and see the Scripture.

The Influence of Rejection

Pray This Prayer Aloud

Lord, I acknowledge that You have been present with me every moment of my life and that You desire to remove the influence of rejection from my life. I acknowledge that rejection sometimes causes me to turn from Your face and wander restlessly. I trust Your heart concerning me, that You want me to enjoy the abundant life and peace You have purchased for me in Christ. I declare that this time in Your presence is holy ground purchased by the blood of Jesus Christ. Therefore, I forbid any distracting influence. I now quiet my mind and choose to focus the eyes of my heart on Your face, trusting You to reveal the source of my rejection. In Your name and presence, Lord Jesus, I pray. Amen.

Focusing on the Presence of God

Do you remember reading about the man who wandered about the tombs in rejection? The Lord spoke to him face-to-face and delivered him from his pain and rejection. Now close your eyes and allow your heart to see the face of Jesus in front of you. Let Him come to you as He came to the man among the tombs and then look deeply into His eyes until every other interfering thought disappears. Allow all other distractions to melt away into the sound of God's gentle stilling. Do not go any further until you have begun to experience the presence of the Lord.

UNCOVERING THE INFLUENCE OF REJECTION

When does rejection control you? Think of a recent or typical event when you felt as though you didn't fit in or belong—a time when your heart wandered alone looking for a place or trying to get attention from others.

Take a few minutes to write a brief description of the event in the space below. What made you feel as though you didn't have a place, that you were wandering, restlessly trying to fit in? Remember that you are still safe in the presence of the Lord as you recall this scene of rejection.

Describe what you were feeling during this event and how you reacted to those feelings. What did you do or want to do to react to this event? If there were any physical sensations associated with this event, make sure to write them down as well (e.g., sweating, accelerated heart rate, pain of any kind, etc.).

Now, pray that the Lord would lead you to the source of those feelings and sensations you experienced during that recent event. The memory He invites you into may look very different from the recent event, but the feelings and reactions will be the same.

> **Prayer:** *Lord, I acknowledge Your presence in every season of my life and that You know where rejection was planted and began to control my heart. I acknowledge that You are still alive in that place and ask You now to invite me there. I declare that I am safe in Your presence even as You lead me to healing. Amen.*

Wait for the Lord to show you where rejection began to control your heart. (Note that there may be more than one memory. Try to determine the memory that stands out the most. Later you will process all the memories brought to light.) The Lord does not always lead us to the first memory but a memory that is most vivid and where He can most easily communicate truth.

Once the Lord has invited you to a memory, it is very important to stand back a few steps and look at it as though you were looking at a painting or a picture in a frame on the wall in front of you. This is important so that you are not so emotionally enmeshed that you cannot experience the presence of the Lord. Be intentional about taking steps back from the memory frame.

Now, describe what you see happening in the picture. (Remember to step back away from the picture.)

As you look into the memory frame, focus on the wounded child in the picture (you at that time). What does that wounded child in the picture feel? Include any physical sensations he/she may have experienced as well. Note things like the posture of the wounded child and his/her general appearance. Describe the child you see in front of you as fully as you can. What does the child in the picture want to do as a result of what is happening and what is he/she feeling as a result? (I remind you again to stand away from the picture and look at it as if looking into a picture frame or perhaps through a window to see the event in front of you.)

Now, why does the child feel what he feels? (The "why" is the lie he believes that causes the rejection.)

"The child in the picture (you at that time) feels _____ because he believes: _____
_____
_____ .

EXPERIENCING THE PRESENCE OF GOD

Prayer: *Lord, by faith I acknowledge Your presence in my pain and ask You to express Your personal presence and heart to comfort the wounded child in the memory frame You have led me to. In Your presence I command all other false voices to silence, and I declare Your sovereign authority over my life. I now wait in Your presence for Your healing truth.*

Describe how you experience the presence of the Lord (i.e., feelings, impressions, images, actions the Lord may take, etc.). This is an act of faith, not imagination. One way to do this is to see the memory frame as a painting with the Lord painting His presence into the scene. You may see an image of the Lord or some other expression of His personal presence. What do you see or sense in the frame? How do you know His presence is there? What is He doing—saying—expressing—gesturing to you as you focus on Him? Again, stand back from the picture frame so that you can see what is happening in front of you.

What does the Lord seem to be communicating to the wounded child in the frame? How do you sense the personal presence of the Lord comforting the wounded child? How do you feel the Lord's interaction with you in a physical sense? Take time to experience the personal presence of the Lord in the memory frame feeling the warmth of His touch or the fragrance of His sweetness. Connect with His presence—body, soul, and spirit. Allow the presence of the Lord to comfort the wounded child in the memory. Is there anything else you sense the Lord communicating?

(DECLARING THE TRUTH)

What is the truth about this situation that the Lord is communicating through the expression of His presence, words, feelings, pictures, etc.?

- **Declaration of Truth:** "I felt *rejection* because I believed _____
  _____
  _____ .

But the truth is [whatever you sense the Lord communicating to that wounded child in the frame] _____
_____
_____ .

I now renounce the lie(s) I came to believe and declare the truth that _____
_____
_____ .

Now that you have received the truth of God, you must "change the locks" so that rejection can no longer move back in to control your life. You "change the locks" by breaking any promises you have made to yourself as a wounded child and by extending forgiveness and removing judgments you have held against those who wounded you.

(CHANGING THE LOCKS)

Renouncing Self-promises

Prayer: *"Lord, I confess to You that I made a promise to myself when I was wounded that I would/would not _____*
_____ . I now break that
promise I made to myself because the truth is _____
_____
_____
Now that I have broken the promise I made to myself, I give
You control of my heart and life."

Extending Forgiveness

To be free of the influence of rejection, you must forgive or receive forgiveness associated with the memory. Forgive and release judgments you have held against those who've wounded you. (Remember that forgiveness is not an act of emotion, but an act of the will so that the pain of that memory can no longer control you.) Speak to them as though you and they are still in that old memory frame. Confess and receive forgiveness for any sin you are responsible for.

> **Prayer:** *Lord, I pray that You bring to my mind any person who I have held judgment or bitterness against because of this wounding event. I choose to see them and myself with Your eyes of compassion and to release any judgment I have held in my heart.*

To receive forgiveness yourself pray...

> **Prayer:** *"Lord, I confess* [any sin you may have committed in the memory the Lord invited you into]. *In this sin I gave legal ground to the enemy of my soul. I now receive forgiveness in the name of Jesus Christ who took this and all my sins upon Himself. I ask You to remove the effects of my sin and restore me to Your presence again.*

To extend mercy and forgiveness, pray...

> **Prayer:** *Lord,* [name the one who wounded you], [tell the Lord what this person or persons did to wound you]. *This wounding caused me to believe* [whatever the lie was that you renounced above] *and to feel* [what the wounded child felt in the memory frame]. *But now, in the presence of the Lord Jesus Christ, I extend grace and forgiveness to them and choose to see them with compassion as You see them.*

Now that you are safe in the presence of the Lord and wrapped in the truth, pause for a moment and look at those who

have wounded you. How do you see them as you bask in the presence of God? What is the truth about them?

I remove all judgments I have held against those who have wounded me and see them as children of God. The truth the Lord has spoken about those who have wounded me is _____

_____

_____ .

Remove demonic strongholds

> **Declaration:** *"Now that I have heard and believe the truth of God which is* [whatever was communicated to the wounded child in the memory frame], *and have forgiven those who wounded me and have removed all judgments I held against them and broken the promise(s) I made to myself; I command all evil and dark spirits who have held lies, judgments, and self-promises in place to depart from me and from my house. You have no legal ground on which to stand.*

> **Prayer:** *Lord, I ask You to now reveal to me any other legal ground I have given to the enemy on which to stand.* [Listen to your heart carefully to see whether or not the Lord may reveal other unfinished business related to this wounding.]

Now ask the Lord to invite you into any other memories with the same feelings and lies, and repeat the process above with each one. You may want to use a separate notebook in which to record these additional memories and the truth the Lord speaks to you in this healing session.

CONTINUING IN THE TRUTH

Now that you have received Truth and healing in the presence of God, it is important to understand that this is only the beginning of healing. Healing is not magical; it is a process. You must continue in the truth and carve new "righteous ruts" for your heart to live in. Refer now to the biblical truths for the various issues in the chapter called "To Be Continued." You may also want to refer to some other topical Bible source to find additional biblical truths that can be applied to your life.

1. Choose a verse from the section "The Healing Truth" relating to rejection in Chapter 15 that stands out to you. Write that verse in the space below.

2. Meditate on the statements. Read the verse several times aloud until you can close your eyes, repeat the Word, and see what the Word is saying to you.[1]

3. As you begin to see this Scripture text in your mind, focus on the presence of the Lord as you sense Him in the Word.

4. Experience the truth in this Scripture, watching and listening for any additional things the Lord may communicate to you personally. You are not changing or adding to the Word but allowing the Lord to continue the conversation.

---

1.   To meditate on the Word, is literally to murmur (from the Hebrew word *hagah*) or repeat the Word or the truth of God to ourselves in a low voice.

5. Now write down/journal whatever you sense is being communicated to you from the Lord in the Scripture text.

6. Repeat the steps above with additional verses from Chapter 15, section "The Healing Truth; Rejection—You Are Accepted in Christ."

WHAT TO DO IF REJECTION IS TRIGGERED AGAIN

1. Go back to the healed memory frame to experience the presence of the Lord.

2. Remind the child in the picture of the presence and the truth of the Lord.

3. Meditate on the scriptural truths that stood out to you, repeating them until you can close your eyes and see the Scripture.

The Influence of Worthlessness

(Pray This Prayer Aloud)

Lord, I acknowledge that You have been present with me every moment of my life and that You desire to remove the influence of worthlessness from my life. I acknowledge that worthlessness sometimes causes me to turn from Your face and strive to earn Your love. I trust Your heart concerning me, that You want me to enjoy the abundant life and peace You have purchased for me in Christ. I declare that this time in Your presence is holy ground purchased by the blood of Jesus Christ. Therefore, I forbid any distracting influence. I now quiet my mind and choose to focus the eyes of my heart on Your face, trusting You to reveal the source of my worthlessness. In Your name and presence, Lord Jesus, I pray. Amen.

(Focusing on the Presence of God)

The Bible tells us that we have been fashioned or molded by the very hand of God (see Ps. 119:73). Closing your eyes, begin to feel the hands of the Lord surrounding you. All that you are flows from His hands and His heart. Feel the gentle pressure of His hand holding and forming you into an object of His great delight. Allow the other distractions to be set aside as you submit to the Creator's gentle touch. Do not continue until you are in the gentle grip of God's loving hands.

Uncovering the Influence of Worthlessness

When does worthlessness control you? Think of a recent or typical event when you felt invisible and unworthy—a time when your heart was telling you to strive and prove your worth—a time when you compared yourself to another person.

Take a few minutes to write a brief description of the event in the space below. What made you want to prove your worth and become visible? Remember that you are still safe in the presence of the Lord as you recall this scene of worthlessness.

Describe what you were feeling during this event and how you reacted to those feelings. What did you do or want to do to react to this event? If there were any physical sensations associated with this event, make sure to write them down as well (e.g., sweating, accelerated heart rate, pain of any kind, etc.).

Now, pray that the Lord would lead you to the source of those feelings and sensations you experienced during that recent event. The memory He invites you into may look very different from the recent event, but the feelings and reactions will be the same.

> **Prayer:** *Lord, I acknowledge Your presence in every season of my life and that You know where worthlessness was planted and began to control my heart. I acknowledge that You are still alive in that place and ask You now to invite me there. I declare that I am safe in Your presence even as You lead me to healing. Amen.*

Wait for the Lord to show you where worthlessness began to control your heart. (Note that there may be more than one memory. Try to determine the memory that stands out the most. Later you will process all the memories brought to light.) The Lord does not always lead us to the first memory but a memory that is most vivid and where He can most easily communicate truth.

Once the Lord has invited you to a memory, it is very important to stand back a few steps and look at it as though you were looking at a painting or a picture in a frame on the wall in front of you. This is important so that you are not so emotionally enmeshed that you cannot experience the presence of the Lord. Be intentional about taking steps back from the memory frame.

Now, describe what you see happening in the picture. (Remember to step back away from the picture.)

As you look into the memory frame, focus on the wounded child in the picture (you at that time). What does that wounded child in the picture feel? Include any physical sensations he/she may have experienced as well. Note things like the posture of the wounded child and his/her general appearance. Describe the child you see in front of you as fully as you can. What does the child in the picture want to do as a result of what is happening and what is he/she feeling as a result? (I remind you again to stand away from the picture and look at it as if looking into a picture frame or perhaps through a window to see the event in front of you.)

Now, why does the child feel what he feels? (The "why" is the lie he believes that causes the worthlessness.)

"The child in the picture (you at that time) feels _____ because he believes: _____

_____

_____ .

(EXPERIENCING THE PRESENCE OF GOD)

Prayer: *Lord, by faith I acknowledge Your presence in my pain and ask You to express Your personal presence and heart to comfort the wounded child in the memory frame You have led me to. In Your presence I command all other false voices to silence, and I declare Your sovereign authority over my life. I now wait in Your presence for Your healing truth.*

Describe how you experience the presence of the Lord (i.e., feelings, impressions, images, actions the Lord may take, etc.). This is an act of faith, not imagination. One way to do this is to see the memory frame as a painting with the Lord painting His presence into the scene. You may see an image of the Lord or some other expression of His personal presence. What do you see or sense in the frame? How do you know His presence is there? What is He doing—saying—expressing—gesturing to you as you focus on Him? Again, stand back from the picture frame so that you can see what is happening in front of you.

What does the Lord seem to be communicating to the wounded child in the frame? How do you sense the personal presence of the Lord comforting the wounded child? How do you feel the Lord's interaction with you in a physical sense? Take time to experience the personal presence of the Lord in the memory frame feeling the warmth of His touch or the fragrance of His sweetness. Connect with His presence—body, soul, and spirit. Allow the presence of the Lord to comfort the wounded child in the memory. Is there anything else you sense the Lord communicating?

DECLARING THE TRUTH

What is the truth about this situation that the Lord is communicating through the expression of His presence, words, feelings, pictures, etc.?

- **Declaration of Truth:** "I felt *worthless* because I believed _____

  _____

  _____ .

But the truth is [whatever you sense the Lord communicating to that wounded child in the frame] _____

_____

_____ .

I now renounce the lie(s) I came to believe and declare the truth that _____

_____

_____ .

Now that you have received the truth of God, you must "change the locks" so that worthlessness can no longer move back in to control your life. You "change the locks" by breaking any promises you have made to yourself as a wounded child and by extending forgiveness and removing judgments you have held against those who wounded you.

CHANGING THE LOCKS

Renouncing Self-promises

Prayer: *"Lord, I confess to You that I made a promise to myself when I was wounded that I would/would not _____*

_____ . I now break that

promise I made to myself because the truth is _____

_____

_____

Now that I have broken the promise I made to myself, I give You control of my heart and life."

Extending Forgiveness

To be free of the influence of worthlessness, you must forgive or receive forgiveness associated with the memory. Forgive and release judgments you have held against those who've wounded you. (Remember that forgiveness is not an act of emotion, but an act of the will so that the pain of that memory can no longer control you.) Speak to them as though you and they are still in that old memory frame. Confess and receive forgiveness for any sin you are responsible for.

> **Prayer:** *Lord, I pray that You bring to my mind any person who I have held judgment or bitterness against because of this wounding event. I choose to see them and myself with Your eyes of compassion and to release any judgment I have held in my heart.*

To receive forgiveness yourself pray…

> **Prayer:** *"Lord, I confess* [any sin you may have committed in the memory the Lord invited you into]. *In this sin I gave legal ground to the enemy of my soul. I now receive forgiveness in the name of Jesus Christ who took this and all my sins upon Himself. I ask You to remove the effects of my sin and restore me to Your presence again.*

To extend mercy and forgiveness, pray…

> **Prayer:** *Lord,* [name the one who wounded you], [tell the Lord what this person or persons did to wound you]. *This wounding caused me to believe* [whatever the lie was that you renounced above] *and to feel* [what the wounded child felt in the memory frame]. *But now, in the presence of the Lord Jesus Christ, I extend grace and forgiveness to them and choose to see them with compassion as You see them.*

Now that you are safe in the presence of the Lord and wrapped in the truth, pause for a moment and look at those who

have wounded you. How do you see them as you bask in the presence of God? What is the truth about them?

I remove all judgments I have held against those who have wounded me and see them as children of God. The truth the Lord has spoken about those who have wounded me is _____

_____

_____.

Remove demonic strongholds

> **Declaration:** *"Now that I have heard and believe the truth of God which is* [whatever was communicated to the wounded child in the memory frame], *and have forgiven those who wounded me and have removed all judgments I held against them and broken the promise(s) I made to myself, I command all evil and dark spirits who have held lies, judgments, and self-promises in place to depart from me and from my house. You have no legal ground on which to stand.*

> **Prayer:** *Lord, I ask You to now reveal to me any other legal ground I have given to the enemy on which to stand.* [Listen to your heart carefully to see whether or not the Lord may reveal other unfinished business related to this wounding.]

Now ask the Lord to invite you into any other memories with the same feelings and lies, and repeat the process above with each one. You may want to use a separate notebook in which to record these additional memories and the truth the Lord speaks to you in this healing session.

(CONTINUING IN THE TRUTH)

Now that you have received Truth and healing in the presence of God, it is important to understand that this is only the beginning of healing. Healing is not magical; it is a process. You must continue in the truth and carve new "righteous ruts" for your heart to live in. Refer now to the biblical truths for the various issues in the chapter called "To Be Continued." You may also want to refer to some other topical Bible source to find additional biblical truths that can be applied to your life.

1. Choose a verse from the section "The Healing Truth" relating to worthlessness in Chapter 15 that stands out to you. Write that verse in the space below.

2. Meditate on the statements. Read the verse several times aloud until you can close your eyes, repeat the Word, and see what the Word is saying to you.[1]

3. As you begin to see this Scripture text in your mind, focus on the presence of the Lord as you sense Him in the Word.

4. Experience the truth in this Scripture, watching and listening for any additional things the Lord may communicate to you personally. You are not changing or adding to the Word but allowing the Lord to continue the conversation.

---

1.   To meditate on the Word, is literally to murmur (from the Hebrew word *hagah*) or repeat the Word or the truth of God to ourselves in a low voice.

5. Now write down/journal whatever you sense is being communicated to you from the Lord in the Scripture text.

6. Repeat the steps above with additional verses from Chapter 15, section "The Healing Truth; Worthlessness—You Are Precious."

WHAT TO DO IF WORTHLESSNESS IS TRIGGERED AGAIN

1. Go back to the healed memory frame to experience the presence of the Lord.

2. Remind the child in the picture of the presence and the truth of the Lord.

3. Meditate on the scriptural truths that stood out to you, repeating them until you can close your eyes and see the Scripture.

THE INFLUENCE OF SHAME

PRAY THIS PRAYER ALOUD

Lord, I acknowledge that You have been present with me every moment of my life and that You desire to remove the influence of shame from my life. I acknowledge that shame sometimes causes me to turn from Your face and hide from You. I trust Your heart concerning me, that You want me to enjoy the abundant life and peace You have purchased for me in Christ. I declare that this time in Your presence is holy ground purchased by the blood of Jesus Christ. Therefore, I forbid any distracting influence. I now quiet my mind and choose to focus the eyes of my heart on Your face, trusting You to reveal the source of my shame. In Your name and presence, Lord Jesus, I pray. Amen.

FOCUSING ON THE PRESENCE OF GOD

Remember in Genesis when Adam and Eve were separated from the face of God and hiding in the bushes? The Lord Himself, knowing all that they had done, came looking for them and said, "Where are you?" Focus on the voice of the Lord who is calling out to you in the same way. Can you hear Him calling, "Where are you?" Close your eyes and quiet your heart as you listen for the sound of God's footsteps coming to look for you. Allow yourself to come out of hiding and into the face of the One who created you.

UNCOVERING THE INFLUENCE OF SHAME

When does shame control you? Think of a recent or typical event when you felt ashamed and exposed—a time when your heart was telling you to hide or cover yourself in some way.

Take a few minutes to write a brief description of the event in the space below. What made you want to hide or cover yourself in some way? Remember that you are still safe in the presence of the Lord as you recall this scene of shame.

Describe what you were feeling during this event and how you reacted to those feelings. What did you do or want to do to react to this event? If there were any physical sensations associated with this event, make sure to write them down as well (e.g., sweating, accelerated heart rate, pain of any kind, etc.).

Now, pray that the Lord would lead you to the source of those feelings and sensations you experienced during that recent event. The memory He invites you into may look very different from the recent event, but the feelings and reactions will be the same.

> **Prayer:** *Lord, I acknowledge Your presence in every season of my life and that You know where shame was planted and began to control my heart. I acknowledge that You are still alive in that place and ask You now to invite me there. I declare that I am safe in Your presence even as You lead me to healing. Amen.*

Wait for the Lord to show you where shame began to control your heart. (Note that there may be more than one memory. Try to determine the memory that stands out the most. Later you will process all the memories brought to light.) The Lord does not always lead us to the first memory but a memory that is most vivid and where He can most easily communicate truth.

Once the Lord has invited you to a memory, it is very important to stand back a few steps and look at it as though you were looking at a painting or a picture in a frame on the wall in front of you. This is important so that you are not so emotionally enmeshed that you cannot experience the presence of the Lord. Be intentional about taking steps back from the memory frame.

Now, describe what you see happening in the picture. (Remember to step back away from the picture.)

As you look into the memory frame, focus on the wounded child in the picture (you at that time). What does that wounded child in the picture feel? Include any physical sensations he/she may have experienced as well. Note things like the posture of the wounded child and his/her general appearance. Describe the child you see in front of you as fully as you can. What does the child in the picture want to do as a result of what is happening and what is he/she feeling as a result? (I remind you again to stand away from the picture and look at it as if looking into a picture frame or perhaps through a window to see the event in front of you.)

Now, why does the child feel what he feels? (The "why" is the lie he believes that causes the shame.)

"The child in the picture (you at that time) feels _____ because he believes: _____
_____
_____ .

EXPERIENCING THE PRESENCE OF GOD

Prayer: *Lord, by faith I acknowledge Your presence in my pain and ask You to express Your personal presence and heart to comfort the wounded child in the memory frame You have led me to. In Your presence I command all other false voices to silence, and I declare Your sovereign authority over my life. I now wait in Your presence for Your healing truth.*

Describe how you experience the presence of the Lord (i.e., feelings, impressions, images, actions the Lord may take, etc.). This is an act of faith, not imagination. One way to do this is to see the memory frame as a painting with the Lord painting His presence into the scene. You may see an image of the Lord or some other expression of His personal presence. What do you see or sense in the frame? How do you know His presence is there? What is He doing—saying—expressing—gesturing to you as you focus on Him? Again, stand back from the picture frame so that you can see what is happening in front of you.

What does the Lord seem to be communicating to the wounded child in the frame? How do you sense the personal presence of the Lord comforting the wounded child? How do you feel the Lord's interaction with you in a physical sense? Take time to experience the personal presence of the Lord in the memory frame feeling the warmth of His touch or the fragrance of His sweetness. Connect with His presence—body, soul, and spirit. Allow the presence of the Lord to comfort the wounded child in the memory. Is there anything else you sense the Lord communicating?

DECLARING THE TRUTH

What is the truth about this situation that the Lord is communicating through the expression of His presence, words, feelings, pictures, etc.?

- **Declaration of Truth:** "I felt *shame* because I believed

_____

_____

_____ .

But the truth is [whatever you sense the Lord communicating to that wounded child in the frame] _____

_____

_____ .

I now renounce the lie(s) I came to believe and declare the truth that _____

_____

_____ .

Now that you have received the truth of God, you must "change the locks" so that shame can no longer move back in to control your life. You "change the locks" by breaking any promises you have made to yourself as a wounded child and by extending forgiveness and removing judgments you have held against those who wounded you.

CHANGING THE LOCKS

Renouncing Self-promises

Prayer: *"Lord, I confess to You that I made a promise to myself when I was wounded that I would/would not _____ _____ . I now break that promise I made to myself because the truth is _____*

_____

_____

Now that I have broken the promise I made to myself, I give You control of my heart and life."

Extending Forgiveness

To be free of the influence of shame, you must forgive or re-ceive forgiveness associated with the memory. Forgive and re-lease judgments you have held against those who've wounded you. (Remember that forgiveness is not an act of emotion, but an act of the will so that the pain of that memory can no longer con-trol you.) Speak to them as though you and they are still in that old memory frame. Confess and receive forgiveness for any sin you are responsible for.

> **Prayer:** *Lord, I pray that You bring to my mind any person who I have held judgment or bitterness against because of this wounding event. I choose to see them and myself with Your eyes of compassion and to release any judgment I have held in my heart.*

To receive forgiveness yourself pray…

> **Prayer:** *"Lord, I confess* [any sin you may have committed in the memory the Lord invited you into]. *In this sin I gave legal ground to the enemy of my soul. I now receive forgive-ness in the name of Jesus Christ who took this and all my sins upon Himself. I ask You to remove the effects of my sin and restore me to Your presence again.*

To extend mercy and forgiveness, pray…

> **Prayer:** *Lord,* [name the one who wounded you], [tell the Lord what this person or persons did to wound you]. *This wounding caused me to believe* [whatever the lie was that you renounced above] *and to feel* [what the wounded child felt in the memory frame]. *But now, in the presence of the Lord Jesus Christ, I extend grace and forgiveness to them and choose to see them with compassion as You see them.*

Now that you are safe in the presence of the Lord and wrapped in the truth, pause for a moment and look at those who

have wounded you. How do you see them as you bask in the presence of God? What is the truth about them?

I remove all judgments I have held against those who have wounded me and see them as children of God. The truth the Lord has spoken about those who have wounded me is _____

_____

_____ .

Remove demonic strongholds

Declaration: "*Now that I have heard and believe the truth of God which is* [whatever was communicated to the wounded child in the memory frame], *and have forgiven those who wounded me and have removed all judgments I held against them and broken the promise(s) I made to myself; I command all evil and dark spirits who have held lies, judgments, and self-promises in place to depart from me and from my house. You have no legal ground on which to stand.*

Prayer: *Lord, I ask You to now reveal to me any other legal ground I have given to the enemy on which to stand.* [Listen to your heart carefully to see whether or not the Lord may reveal other unfinished business related to this wounding.]

Now ask the Lord to invite you into any other memories with the same feelings and lies, and repeat the process above with each one. You may want to use a separate notebook in which to record these additional memories and the truth the Lord speaks to you in this healing session.

CONTINUING IN THE TRUTH

Now that you have received Truth and healing in the presence of God, it is important to understand that this is only the beginning of healing. Healing is not magical; it is a process. You must continue in the truth and carve new "righteous ruts" for your heart to live in. Refer now to the biblical truths for the various issues in the chapter called "To Be Continued." You may also want to refer to some other topical Bible source to find additional biblical truths that can be applied to your life.

1. Choose a verse from the section "The Healing Truth" relating to shame in Chapter 15 that stands out to you. Write that verse in the space below.

2. Meditate on the statements. Read the verse several times aloud until you can close your eyes, repeat the Word, and see what the Word is saying to you.[1]

3. As you begin to see this Scripture text in your mind, focus on the presence of the Lord as you sense Him in the Word.

4. Experience the truth in this Scripture, watching and listening for any additional things the Lord may communicate to you personally. You are not changing or adding to the Word but allowing the Lord to continue the conversation.

---

1. To meditate on the Word, is literally to murmur (from the Hebrew word *hagah*) or repeat the Word or the truth of God to ourselves in a low voice.

5. Now write down/journal whatever you sense is being communicated to you from the Lord in the Scripture text.

6. Repeat the steps above with additional verses from Chapter 15, section "The Healing Truth; Shame—You Are Covered in Christ."

What to Do if Shame Is Triggered Again

1. Go back to the healed memory frame to experience the presence of the Lord.

2. Remind the child in the picture of the presence and the truth of the Lord.

3. Meditate on the scriptural truths that stood out to you, repeating them until you can close your eyes and see the Scripture.

THE INFLUENCE OF INSECURITY

(PRAY THIS PRAYER ALOUD)

Lord, I acknowledge that You have been present with me every moment of my life and that You desire to remove the influence of insecurity from my life. I acknowledge that insecurity sometimes causes me to try to take control of my own life. I trust Your heart concerning me, that You want me to enjoy the abundant life and peace You have purchased for me in Christ. I declare that this time in Your presence is holy ground purchased by the blood of Jesus Christ. Therefore, I forbid any distracting influence. I now quiet my mind and choose to focus the eyes of my heart on Your face, trusting You to reveal the source of my insecurity. In Your name and presence, Lord Jesus, I pray. Amen.

(FOCUSING ON THE PRESENCE OF GOD)

Do you recall the scene when Mephibosheth was brought into the presence of King David? Ultimately he was taken to the table of the king to live in his presence. We too have been invited to the King's table. Close your eyes and allow yourself to be seated at the table with the King. Focus on His face as you relax in this place of ultimate security and safety. Do not proceed until you can rest at the table of the King.

UNCOVERING THE INFLUENCE OF INSECURITY

When does insecurity control you? Think of a recent or typical event when you felt threatened or trapped—a time when your heart was telling you to take control somehow or withdraw to a safer place.

Take a few minutes to write a brief description of the event in the space below. What made you want to run away or avoid this person or circumstance? Remember that you are still safe in the presence of the Lord as you recall this scene of insecurity.

Describe what you were feeling during this event and how you reacted to those feelings. What did you do or want to do to react to this event? If there were any physical sensations associated with this event, make sure to write them down as well (e.g., sweating, accelerated heart rate, pain of any kind, etc.).

Now, pray that the Lord would lead you to the source of those feelings and sensations you experienced during that recent event. The memory He invites you into may look very different from the recent event, but the feelings and reactions will be the same.

> **Prayer:** *Lord, I acknowledge Your presence in every season of my life and that You know where insecurity was planted and began to control my heart. I acknowledge that You are still alive in that place and ask You now to invite me there. I declare that I am safe in Your presence even as You lead me to healing. Amen.*

Wait for the Lord to show you where insecurity began to control your heart. (Note that there may be more than one memory. Try to determine the memory that stands out the most. Later you will process all the memories brought to light.) The Lord does not always lead us to the first memory but a memory that is most vivid and where He can most easily communicate truth.

Once the Lord has invited you to a memory, it is very important to stand back a few steps and look at it as though you were looking at a painting or a picture in a frame on the wall in front of you. This is important so that you are not so emotionally enmeshed that you cannot experience the presence of the Lord. Be intentional about taking steps back from the memory frame.

Now, describe what you see happening in the picture. (Remember to step back away from the picture.)

As you look into the memory frame, focus on the wounded child in the picture (you at that time). What does that wounded child in the picture feel? Include any physical sensations he/she may have experienced as well. Note things like the posture of the wounded child and his/her general appearance. Describe the child you see in front of you as fully as you can. What does the child in the picture want to do as a result of what is happening and what is he/she feeling as a result? (I remind you again to stand away from the picture and look at it as if looking into a picture frame or perhaps through a window to see the event in front of you.)

Now, why does the child feel what he feels? (The "why" is the lie he believes that causes the insecurity.)

"The child in the picture (you at that time) feels _____ because he believes: _____

_____

_____.

(EXPERIENCING THE PRESENCE OF GOD)

Prayer: *Lord, by faith I acknowledge Your presence in my pain and ask You to express Your personal presence and heart to comfort the wounded child in the memory frame You have led me to. In Your presence I command all other false voices to silence, and I declare Your sovereign authority over my life. I now wait in Your presence for Your healing truth.*

Describe how you experience the presence of the Lord (i.e., feelings, impressions, images, actions the Lord may take, etc.). This is an act of faith, not imagination. One way to do this is to see the memory frame as a painting with the Lord painting His presence into the scene. You may see an image of the Lord or some other expression of His personal presence. What do you see or sense in the frame? How do you know His presence is there? What is He doing—saying—expressing—gesturing to you as you focus on Him? Again, stand back from the picture frame so that you can see what is happening in front of you.

What does the Lord seem to be communicating to the wounded child in the frame? How do you sense the personal presence of the Lord comforting the wounded child? How do you feel the Lord's interaction with you in a physical sense? Take time to experience the personal presence of the Lord in the memory frame feeling the warmth of His touch or the fragrance of His sweetness. Connect with His presence—body, soul, and spirit. Allow the presence of the Lord to comfort the wounded child in the memory. Is there anything else you sense the Lord communicating?

DECLARING THE TRUTH

What is the truth about this situation that the Lord is communicating through the expression of His presence, words, feelings, pictures, etc.?

- **Declaration of Truth:** "I felt *insecure* because I believed _____
_____
_____ .

But the truth is [whatever you sense the Lord communicating to that wounded child in the frame] _____
_____
_____ .

I now renounce the lie(s) I came to believe and declare the truth that _____
_____
_____ .

Now that you have received the truth of God, you must "change the locks" so that insecurity can no longer move back in to control your life. You "change the locks" by breaking any promises you have made to yourself as a wounded child and by extending forgiveness and removing judgments you have held against those who wounded you.

CHANGING THE LOCKS

Renouncing Self-promises

Prayer: *"Lord, I confess to You that I made a promise to myself when I was wounded that I would/would not _____
_____ . I now break that promise I made to myself because the truth is _____
_____
_____
Now that I have broken the promise I made to myself, I give You control of my heart and life."*

Extending Forgiveness

To be free of the influence of insecurity, you must forgive or receive forgiveness associated with the memory. Forgive and release judgments you have held against those who've wounded you. (Remember that forgiveness is not an act of emotion, but an act of the will so that the pain of that memory can no longer control you.) Speak to them as though you and they are still in that old memory frame. Confess and receive forgiveness for any sin you are responsible for.

> **Prayer:** *Lord, I pray that You bring to my mind any person who I have held judgment or bitterness against because of this wounding event. I choose to see them and myself with Your eyes of compassion and to release any judgment I have held in my heart.*

To receive forgiveness yourself pray...

> **Prayer:** *"Lord, I confess* [any sin you may have committed in the memory the Lord invited you into]. *In this sin I gave legal ground to the enemy of my soul. I now receive forgiveness in the name of Jesus Christ who took this and all my sins upon Himself. I ask You to remove the effects of my sin and restore me to Your presence again.*

To extend mercy and forgiveness, pray...

> **Prayer:** *Lord,* [name the one who wounded you], [tell the Lord what this person or persons did to wound you]. *This wounding caused me to believe* [whatever the lie was that you renounced above] *and to feel* [what the wounded child felt in the memory frame]. *But now, in the presence of the Lord Jesus Christ, I extend grace and forgiveness to them and choose to see them with compassion as You see them.*

Now that you are safe in the presence of the Lord and wrapped in the truth, pause for a moment and look at those who

have wounded you. How do you see them as you bask in the presence of God? What is the truth about them?

I remove all judgments I have held against those who have wounded me and see them as children of God. The truth the Lord has spoken about those who have wounded me is _____

_____

_____.

Remove demonic strongholds

Declaration: *"Now that I have heard and believe the truth of God which is* [whatever was communicated to the wounded child in the memory frame]*, and have forgiven those who wounded me and have removed all judgments I held against them and broken the promise(s) I made to myself; I command all evil and dark spirits who have held lies, judgments, and self-promises in place to depart from me and from my house. You have no legal ground on which to stand.*

Prayer: *Lord, I ask You to now reveal to me any other legal ground I have given to the enemy on which to stand.* [Listen to your heart carefully to see whether or not the Lord may reveal other unfinished business related to this wounding.]

Now ask the Lord to invite you into any other memories with the same feelings and lies, and repeat the process above with each one. You may want to use a separate notebook in which to record these additional memories and the truth the Lord speaks to you in this healing session.

CONTINUING IN THE TRUTH

Now that you have received Truth and healing in the presence of God, it is important to understand that this is only the beginning of healing. Healing is not magical; it is a process. You must continue in the truth and carve new "righteous ruts" for your heart to live in. Refer now to the biblical truths for the various issues in the chapter called "To Be Continued." You may also want to refer to some other topical Bible source to find additional biblical truths that can be applied to your life.

1. Choose a verse from the section "The Healing Truth" relating to insecurity in Chapter 15 that stands out to you. Write that verse in the space below.

2. Meditate on the statements. Read the verse several times aloud until you can close your eyes, repeat the Word, and see what the Word is saying to you.[1]

3. As you begin to see this Scripture text in your mind, focus on the presence of the Lord as you sense Him in the Word.

4. Experience the truth in this Scripture, watching and listening for any additional things the Lord may communicate to you personally. You are not changing or adding to the Word but allowing the Lord to continue the conversation.

---

1.   To meditate on the Word, is literally to murmur (from the Hebrew word *hagah*) or repeat the Word or the truth of God to ourselves in a low voice.

5. Now write down/journal whatever you sense is being communicated to you from the Lord in the Scripture text.

6. Repeat the steps above with additional verses from Chapter 15, section "The Healing Truth; Insecurity—You Are Safe in Christ."

WHAT TO DO IF INSECURITY IS TRIGGERED AGAIN

1. Go back to the healed memory frame to experience the presence of the Lord.

2. Remind the child in the picture of the presence and the truth of the Lord.

3. Meditate on the scriptural truths that stood out to you, repeating them until you can close your eyes and see the Scripture.

THE INFLUENCE OF DEFILEMENT

PRAY THIS PRAYER ALOUD

Lord, I acknowledge that You have been present with me every moment of my life and that You desire to remove the influence of defilement from my life. I acknowledge that defilement sometimes causes me to turn from Your face and wear the shame of what some one else did to me. I trust Your heart concerning me, that You want me to enjoy the abundant life and peace You have purchased for me in Christ. I declare that this time in Your presence is holy ground purchased by the blood of Jesus Christ. Therefore, I forbid any distracting influence. I now quiet my mind and choose to focus the eyes of my heart on Your face, trusting You to reveal the source of my defilement. In Your name and presence, Lord Jesus, I pray. Amen.

FOCUSING ON THE PRESENCE OF GOD

The world can be a noisy and chaotic place, but a quiet place is available in the heart of the Father. Remember that the Lord has seen every day of your life and each wound you have received. In the day of your wounding, He saw the day of your healing—even this very moment as you read these words. He is with you in this present moment. He has led and invited you to quiet your heart as you rest between His hands. Pause now and see yourself in this place of ultimate acceptance and restoration.

UNCOVERING THE INFLUENCE OF DEFILEMENT

When does the influence of defilement control you? Think of a recent or typical event when you felt dirty or unclean—a time when your heart was telling you to recoil from intimacy—that you were somehow spoiled goods.

Take a few minutes to write a brief description of the event in the space below. What is it that you cannot get past—that makes you feel dirty or empty inside? Remember that you are still safe in the presence of the Lord as you recall this scene of defilement.

Describe what you were feeling during this event and how you reacted to those feelings. What did you do or want to do to react to this event? If there were any physical sensations associated with this event, make sure to write them down as well (e.g., sweating, accelerated heart rate, pain of any kind, etc.).

Now, pray that the Lord would lead you to the source of those feelings and sensations you experienced during that recent event. The memory He invites you into may look very different from the recent event, but the feelings and reactions will be the same.

> **Prayer:** *Lord, I acknowledge Your presence in every season of my life and that You know where defilement was planted and began to control my heart. I acknowledge that You are still alive in that place and ask You now to invite me there. I declare that I am safe in Your presence even as You lead me to healing. Amen.*

Wait for the Lord to show you where defilement began to control your heart. (Note that there may be more than one memory. Try to determine the memory that stands out the most. Later you will process all the memories brought to light.) The Lord does not always lead us to the first memory but a memory that is most vivid and where He can most easily communicate truth.

Once the Lord has invited you to a memory, it is very important to stand back a few steps and look at it as though you were looking at a painting or a picture in a frame on the wall in front of you. This is important so that you are not so emotionally enmeshed that you cannot experience the presence of the Lord. Be intentional about taking steps back from the memory frame.

Now, describe what you see happening in the picture. (Remember to step back away from the picture.)

As you look into the memory frame, focus on the wounded child in the picture (you at that time). What does that wounded child in the picture feel? Include any physical sensations he/she may have experienced as well. Note things like the posture of the wounded child and his/her general appearance. Describe the child you see in front of you as fully as you can. What does the child in the picture want to do as a result of what is happening and what is he/she feeling as a result? (I remind you again to stand away from the picture and look at it as if looking into a picture frame or perhaps through a window to see the event in front of you.)

Now, why does the child feel what he feels? (The "why" is the lie he believes that causes the feeling of defilement.)

"The child in the picture (you at that time) feels _____ because he believes: _____
_____
_____.

┌───┐
(EXPERIENCING THE PRESENCE OF GOD)
└───┘

Prayer: *Lord, by faith I acknowledge Your presence in my pain and ask You to express Your personal presence and heart to comfort the wounded child in the memory frame You have led me to. In Your presence I command all other false voices to silence, and I declare Your sovereign authority over my life. I now wait in Your presence for Your healing truth.*

Describe how you experience the presence of the Lord (i.e., feelings, impressions, images, actions the Lord may take, etc.). This is an act of faith, not imagination. One way to do this is to see the memory frame as a painting with the Lord painting His presence into the scene. You may see an image of the Lord or some other expression of His personal presence. What do you see or sense in the frame? How do you know His presence is there? What is He doing—saying—expressing—gesturing to you as you focus on Him? Again, stand back from the picture frame so that you can see what is happening in front of you.

What does the Lord seem to be communicating to the wounded child in the frame? How do you sense the personal presence of the Lord comforting the wounded child? How do you feel the Lord's interaction with you in a physical sense? Take time to experience the personal presence of the Lord in the memory frame feeling the warmth of His touch or the fragrance of His sweetness. Connect with His presence—body, soul, and spirit. Allow the presence of the Lord to comfort the wounded child in the memory. Is there anything else you sense the Lord communicating?

DECLARING THE TRUTH

What is the truth about this situation that the Lord is communicating through the expression of His presence, words, feelings, pictures, etc.?

- **Declaration of Truth:** "I felt *defiled* because I believed _____

_____

_____ .

But the truth is [whatever you sense the Lord communicating to that wounded child in the frame] _____

_____

_____ .

I now renounce the lie(s) I came to believe and declare the truth that _____

_____

_____ .

Now that you have received the truth of God, you must "change the locks" so that defilement can no longer move back in to control your life. You "change the locks" by breaking any promises you have made to yourself as a wounded child and by extending forgiveness and removing judgments you have held against those who wounded you.

CHANGING THE LOCKS

Renouncing Self-promises

Prayer: *"Lord, I confess to You that I made a promise to myself when I was wounded that I would/would not _____*

_____ . I now break that promise I made to myself because the truth is _____

_____

_____

Now that I have broken the promise I made to myself, I give You control of my heart and life."

Extending Forgiveness

To be free of the influence of defilement, you must forgive or receive forgiveness associated with the memory. Forgive and release judgments you have held against those who've wounded you. (Remember that forgiveness is not an act of emotion, but an act of the will so that the pain of that memory can no longer control you.) Speak to them as though you and they are still in that old memory frame. Confess and receive forgiveness for any sin you are responsible for.

> **Prayer:** *Lord, I pray that You bring to my mind any person who I have held judgment or bitterness against because of this wounding event. I choose to see them and myself with Your eyes of compassion and to release any judgment I have held in my heart.*

To receive forgiveness yourself pray...

> **Prayer:** *"Lord, I confess [any sin you may have committed in the memory the Lord invited you into]. In this sin I gave legal ground to the enemy of my soul. I now receive forgiveness in the name of Jesus Christ who took this and all my sins upon Himself. I ask You to remove the effects of my sin and restore me to Your presence again.*

To extend mercy and forgiveness, pray...

> **Prayer:** *Lord, [name the one who wounded you], [tell the Lord what this person or persons did to wound you]. This wounding caused me to believe [whatever the lie was that you renounced above] and to feel [what the wounded child felt in the memory frame]. But now, in the presence of the Lord Jesus Christ, I extend grace and forgiveness to them and choose to see them with compassion as You see them.*

Now that you are safe in the presence of the Lord and wrapped in the truth, pause for a moment and look at those who

have wounded you. How do you see them as you bask in the presence of God? What is the truth about them?

I remove all judgments I have held against those who have wounded me and see them as children of God. The truth the Lord has spoken about those who have wounded me is _____
_____
_____.

Remove demonic strongholds

Declaration: "*Now that I have heard and believe the truth of God which is* [whatever was communicated to the wounded child in the memory frame], *and have forgiven those who wounded me and have removed all judgments I held against them and broken the promise(s) I made to myself; I command all evil and dark spirits who have held lies, judgments, and self-promises in place to depart from me and from my house. You have no legal ground on which to stand.*

Prayer: *Lord, I ask You to now reveal to me any other legal ground I have given to the enemy on which to stand.* [Listen to your heart carefully to see whether or not the Lord may reveal other unfinished business related to this wounding.]

Now ask the Lord to invite you into any other memories with the same feelings and lies, and repeat the process above with each one. You may want to use a separate notebook in which to record these additional memories and the truth the Lord speaks to you in this healing session.

CONTINUING IN THE TRUTH

Now that you have received Truth and healing in the presence of God, it is important to understand that this is only the beginning of healing. Healing is not magical; it is a process. You must continue in the truth and carve new "righteous ruts" for your heart to live in. Refer now to the biblical truths for the various issues in the chapter called "To Be Continued." You may also want to refer to some other topical Bible source to find additional biblical truths that can be applied to your life.

1. Choose a verse from the section "The Healing Truth" relating to defilement in Chapter 15 that stands out to you. Write that verse in the space below.

2. Meditate on the statements. Read the verse several times aloud until you can close your eyes, repeat the Word, and see what the Word is saying to you.[1]

3. As you begin to see this Scripture text in your mind, focus on the presence of the Lord as you sense Him in the Word.

4. Experience the truth in this Scripture, watching and listening for any additional things the Lord may communicate to you personally. You are not changing or adding to the Word but allowing the Lord to continue the conversation.

---

1. To meditate on the Word, is literally to murmur (from the Hebrew word *hagah*) or repeat the Word or the truth of God to ourselves in a low voice.

5. Now write down/journal whatever you sense is being communicated to you from the Lord in the Scripture text.

6. Repeat the steps above with additional verses from Chapter 15, section "The Healing Truth; Defilement—You Are Restored in Christ Jesus."

WHAT TO DO IF DEFILEMENT IS TRIGGERED AGAIN

1. Go back to the healed memory frame to experience the presence of the Lord.

2. Remind the child in the picture of the presence and the truth of the Lord.

3. Meditate on the scriptural truths that stood out to you, repeating them until you can close your eyes and see the Scripture.

THE INFLUENCE OF HOPELESSNESS

PRAY THIS PRAYER ALOUD

Lord, I acknowledge that You have been present with me every moment of my life and that You desire to remove the influence of hopelessness from my life. I acknowledge that hopelessness sometimes causes me to turn from Your face and quit. I trust Your heart concerning me, that You want me to enjoy the abundant life and peace You have purchased for me in Christ. I declare that this time in Your presence is holy ground purchased by the blood of Jesus Christ. Therefore, I forbid any distracting influence. I now quiet my mind and choose to focus the eyes of my heart on Your face, trusting You to reveal the source of my hopelessness. In Your name and presence, Lord Jesus, I pray. Amen.

FOCUSING ON THE PRESENCE OF GOD

Do you remember when Mary Magdelene heard the Lord Jesus speak her name? She turned around and threw herself at His feet. Will you now close your eyes, quiet your heart, and allow the Lord to speak your name? Allow the other distractions to melt away into the sound of your own name being spoken softly by the Lord. Do not go any further until you have begun to experience the presence of the Lord.

UNCOVERING THE INFLUENCE OF HOPELESSNESS

When does the hopelessness control you? Think of a recent or typical event when you felt hopeless—a time when your heart was telling you to sit down and quit.

Take a few minutes to write a brief description of the event in the space below. What made you want to stop moving or to see no way to go on? Remember that you are still safe in the presence of the Lord as you recall this scene of hopelessness.

Describe what you were feeling during this event and how you reacted to those feelings. What did you do or want to do to react to this event? If there were any physical sensations associated with this event, make sure to write them down as well (e.g., sweating, accelerated heart rate, pain of any kind, etc.).

Now, pray that the Lord would lead you to the source of those feelings and sensations you experienced during that recent event. The memory He invites you into may look very different from the recent event, but the feelings and reactions will be the same.

> **Prayer:** *Lord, I acknowledge Your presence in every season of my life and that You know where hopelessness was planted and began to control my heart. I acknowledge that You are still alive in that place and ask You now to invite me there. I declare that I am safe in Your presence even as You lead me to healing. Amen.*

Wait for the Lord to show you where hopelessness began to control your heart. (Note that there may be more than one memory. Try to determine the memory that stands out the most. Later you will process all the memories brought to light.) The Lord does not always lead us to the first memory but a memory that is most vivid and where He can most easily communicate truth.

Once the Lord has invited you to a memory, it is very important to stand back a few steps and look at it as though you were looking at a painting or a picture in a frame on the wall in front of you. This is important so that you are not so emotionally enmeshed that you cannot experience the presence of the Lord. Be intentional about taking steps back from the memory frame.

Now, describe what you see happening in the picture. (Remember to step back away from the picture.)

As you look into the memory frame, focus on the wounded child in the picture (you at that time). What does that wounded child in the picture feel? Include any physical sensations he/she may have experienced as well. Note things like the posture of the wounded child and his/her general appearance. Describe the child you see in front of you as fully as you can. What does the child in the picture want to do as a result of what is happening and what is he/she feeling as a result? (I remind you again to stand away from the picture and look at it as if looking into a picture frame or perhaps through a window to see the event in front of you.)

Now, why does the child feel what he feels? (The "why" is the lie he believes that causes the hopelessness.)

"The child in the picture (you at that time) feels _____ because he believes: _____

_____

_____ .

EXPERIENCING THE PRESENCE OF GOD

Prayer: *Lord, by faith I acknowledge Your presence in my pain and ask You to express Your personal presence and heart to comfort the wounded child in the memory frame You have led me to. In Your presence I command all other false voices to silence, and I declare Your sovereign authority over my life. I now wait in Your presence for Your healing truth.*

Describe how you experience the presence of the Lord (i.e., feelings, impressions, images, actions the Lord may take, etc.). This is an act of faith, not imagination. One way to do this is to see the memory frame as a painting with the Lord painting His presence into the scene. You may see an image of the Lord or some other expression of His personal presence. What do you see or sense in the frame? How do you know His presence is there? What is He doing—saying—expressing—gesturing to you as you focus on Him? Again, stand back from the picture frame so that you can see what is happening in front of you.

What does the Lord seem to be communicating to the wounded child in the frame? How do you sense the personal presence of the Lord comforting the wounded child? How do you feel the Lord's interaction with you in a physical sense? Take time to experience the personal presence of the Lord in the memory frame feeling the warmth of His touch or the fragrance of His sweetness. Connect with His presence—body, soul, and spirit. Allow the presence of the Lord to comfort the wounded child in the memory. Is there anything else you sense the Lord communicating?

DECLARING THE TRUTH

What is the truth about this situation that the Lord is communicating through the expression of His presence, words, feelings, pictures, etc.?

- **Declaration of Truth:** "I felt *hopeless* because I believed _____
_____
_____ .

But the truth is [whatever you sense the Lord communicating to that wounded child in the frame] _____
_____
_____ .

I now renounce the lie(s) I came to believe and declare the truth that _____
_____
_____ .

Now that you have received the truth of God, you must "change the locks" so that hopelessness can no longer move back in to control your life. You "change the locks" by breaking any promises you have made to yourself as a wounded child and by extending forgiveness and removing judgments you have held against those who wounded you.

CHANGING THE LOCKS

Renouncing Self-promises

Prayer: *"Lord, I confess to You that I made a promise to myself when I was wounded that I would/would not _____*
_____ . I now break that
promise I made to myself because the truth is _____
_____
_____

Now that I have broken the promise I made to myself, I give You control of my heart and life."

Extending Forgiveness

To be free of the influence of hopelessness, you must forgive or receive forgiveness associated with the memory. Forgive and release judgments you have held against those who've wounded you. (Remember that forgiveness is not an act of emotion, but an act of the will so that the pain of that memory can no longer control you.) Speak to them as though you and they are still in that old memory frame. Confess and receive forgiveness for any sin you are responsible for.

> **Prayer:** *Lord, I pray that You bring to my mind any person who I have held judgment or bitterness against because of this wounding event. I choose to see them and myself with Your eyes of compassion and to release any judgment I have held in my heart.*

To receive forgiveness yourself pray...

> **Prayer:** *"Lord, I confess* [any sin you may have committed in the memory the Lord invited you into]. *In this sin I gave legal ground to the enemy of my soul. I now receive forgiveness in the name of Jesus Christ who took this and all my sins upon Himself. I ask You to remove the effects of my sin and restore me to Your presence again.*

To extend mercy and forgiveness, pray...

> **Prayer:** *Lord,* [name the one who wounded you], [tell the Lord what this person or persons did to wound you]. *This wounding caused me to believe* [whatever the lie was that you renounced above] *and to feel* [what the wounded child felt in the memory frame]. *But now, in the presence of the Lord Jesus Christ, I extend grace and forgiveness to them and choose to see them with compassion as You see them.*

Now that you are safe in the presence of the Lord and wrapped in the truth, pause for a moment and look at those who

have wounded you. How do you see them as you bask in the presence of God? What is the truth about them?

I remove all judgments I have held against those who have wounded me and see them as children of God. The truth the Lord has spoken about those who have wounded me is _____

_____

_____.

Remove demonic strongholds

Declaration: "*Now that I have heard and believe the truth of God which is* [whatever was communicated to the wounded child in the memory frame], *and have forgiven those who wounded me and have removed all judgments I held against them and broken the promise(s) I made to myself; I command all evil and dark spirits who have held lies, judgments, and self-promises in place to depart from me and from my house. You have no legal ground on which to stand.*

Prayer: *Lord, I ask You to now reveal to me any other legal ground I have given to the enemy on which to stand.* [Listen to your heart carefully to see whether or not the Lord may reveal other unfinished business related to this wounding.]

Now ask the Lord to invite you into any other memories with the same feelings and lies, and repeat the process above with each one. You may want to use a separate notebook in which to record these additional memories and the truth the Lord speaks to you in this healing session.

CONTINUING IN THE TRUTH

Now that you have received Truth and healing in the presence of God, it is important to understand that this is only the beginning of healing. Healing is not magical; it is a process. You must continue in the truth and carve new "righteous ruts" for your heart to live in. Refer now to the biblical truths for the various issues in the chapter called "To Be Continued." You may also want to refer to some other topical Bible source to find additional biblical truths that can be applied to your life.

1. Choose a verse from the section "The Healing Truth" relating to hopelessness in Chapter 15 that stands out to you. Write that verse in the space below.

2. Meditate on the statements. Read the verse several times aloud until you can close your eyes, repeat the Word, and see what the Word is saying to you.[1]

3. As you begin to see this Scripture text in your mind, focus on the presence of the Lord as you sense Him in the Word.

4. Experience the truth in this Scripture, watching and listening for any additional things the Lord may communicate to you personally. You are not changing or adding to the Word but allowing the Lord to continue the conversation.

---

1.   To meditate on the Word, is literally to murmur (from the Hebrew word *hagah*) or repeat the Word or the truth of God to ourselves in a low voice.

5. Now write down/journal whatever you sense is being communicated to you from the Lord in the Scripture text.

6. Repeat the steps above with additional verses from Chapter 15, section "The Healing Truth; Hopelessness—You Have a Living Hope in Christ Jesus."

What to Do if Hopelessness Is Triggered Again

1. Go back to the healed memory frame to experience the presence of the Lord.

2. Remind the child in the picture of the presence and the truth of the Lord.

3. Meditate on the scriptural truths that stood out to you, repeating them until you can close your eyes and see the Scripture.

REFERENCES

Biblesoft's New Exhaustive Strong's Numbers and Concordance with Expanded Greek-Hebrew Dictionary. 1994. Biblesoft and International Bible Translators, Inc.

Crabb, Larry. 1977. *Effective Biblical Counseling.* Grand Rapids, MI: Zondervan Publishing House.

Flynn, Mike, and Doug Gregg. 1993. *Inner Healing.* Downers Grove, IL: Intervarsity Press.

Kraft, Charles H. 1993. *Deep Wounds, Deep Healing.* Ann Arbor, MI: Servant Pub.

Long, Brad, and Cindy Strickler. 2001. *Let Jesus Heal Your Hidden Wounds.* Grand Rapids, MI: Chosen Books.

Petersen, Alice; Gary Sweeten; and Dorothy Faye Geverdt. 1990. "Renewing Mind." *Rational Christian Thinking.* Cincinnati: Equipping Ministries Int'l.

Sandford, John, and Paula Sandford. 1985. *Healing the Wounded Spirit.* Tulsa, OK: Victory House, Inc.

Sandford, John Loren, and Mark Sandford. 1992. *A Comprehensive Guide to Deliverance and Healing.* Grand Rapids, MI: Chosen Books.

Seamands, David A. 1985. *Healing of Memories.* Colorado Springs, CO: Chariot Victor Pub.

Smith, Edward M. 2002. *Beyond Tolerable Recovery.* Campbellsville, KY: Family Care Pub.

MINISTRY INFORMATION

The mission of Grace and Truth Fellowship, Inc., is to transform local churches into healing centers. Serving as president of this ministry, Thom Gardner is available as a speaker/teacher for seminars, conferences, or other extended meetings. Grace and Truth Fellowship, Inc., also offers the *Healing the Wounded Heart Training Seminar* to equip the local church to bring healing to wounded hearts. The purpose of the seminar is to help participants find personal freedom through confrontation of their own past wounds, and then equip them to bring healing to others.

Healing the Wounded Heart Training Seminar is a three-day seminar that covers the material in this book and offers instruction and practice in the facilitation of this approach to healing wounded hearts. Our goal is to multiply, rather than monopolize, this approach to the ministry of inner healing.

If you are interested in attending a *Healing the Wounded Heart Training Seminar*, contact Grace and Truth Fellowship, Inc., at 717-263-6869, or see our web site at www.grace andtruthfellowship.com.

Additional copies of this book and other book titles from DESTINY IMAGE are available at your local bookstore.

For a complete list of our titles, visit us at www.destinyimage.com Send a request for a catalog to:

Destiny Image® Publishers, Inc.
P.O. Box 310
Shippensburg, PA 17257-0310

*"Speaking to the Purposes of God for This
Generation and for the Generations to Come"*